SULPHUR AND MOLASSES

SULPHUR AND MOLASSES

Home Remedies and Other Echoes of the Canadian Past

by Audrey Armstrong

MUSSON BOOK COMPANY
Don Mills, Ontario

First published in 1977 by
Musson Book Company
30 Lesmill Road, Don Mills, Ontario

ISBN 0-7737-1013-2

Canadian Cataloguing in Publication Data
Armstrong, Audrey I., 1920-
Sulphur & molasses
ISBN 0-7737-1013-2 pa.
1. Canada – Social life and customs. 2. Frontier and pioneer life – Canada. 3. Folk-lore – Canada.
I. Title.
FC85.A76 971 C77-001263-9
F1021.A76

Printed in Canada

Design/Peter Maher

Illustrations/J. Merle Smith

First printing

To Wib

Acknowledgments

My friends and neighbours, relatives and acquaintances, and many visitors to Black Creek Pioneer Village - where for several years I portrayed Mrs. Flynn - all contributed to *Sulphur and Molasses*. For anecdotes about family and farm life, for descriptions of home remedies - herbal, medicinal and non-medical, for old-time "receipts", and miscellaneous information, I offer my sincere thanks.

Assistance from the Ontario Arts Council made it possible for me to take the time to research this book. A patient publisher put together a fine team to produce it; illustrator Merle Smith, designer Peter Maher, and photographer Peter Paterson combined their talents to make this an attractive volume. And my family gave me continual support and encouragement during the months when the manuscript was in progress. Without all of these people, *Sulphur and Molasses* might have been left untouched on the old wood-burning stove.

Contents

Preface

Life has changed dramatically in many ways since the so-called horse-and-buggy days, and we usually like to think that most of the changes have been for the better. Everyday household tasks which used to take hours can now be done easily and quickly with the aid of the marvellous range of labour-saving devices that most of us take for granted. Skilled doctors and well-equipped hospitals are within easy reach of most Canadians, and miracle drugs have almost eliminated many dreaded diseases.

But many people fondly remember a simpler time, when life held fewer decisions and the pressures of daily living were perhaps not quite as overpowering as they sometimes seem today. Some modern pioneers, drawn to the more self-sufficient ways of earlier times, have chosen to leave the questionable comforts of the city to go "back to the land" and simplify their existence. I offer this book to those who feel that the past has something of value for the present, to those for whom the gentler times hold a certain appeal.

My own memories of my childhood and youth on an Ottawa Valley farm are always with me. I remember one Christmas night when I was driven over bumpy, unplowed winter roads in a horse-drawn sleigh to an Ottawa hospital, to be relieved of what our family doctor described as a red-hot appendix. Like many others, I recall the questionable comfort obtained from home remedies when no doctor was at hand to prescribe more scientific treatment. And I recollect the coming of spring, when the flow of the icy streams, swollen with the melting snow, was accompanied by the inevitable spring tonic.

Winnifred Horne of Ottawa has described the transition delightfully when she wrote:

It's candy-coloured capsules now
With vitamins required
For winter-weary little ones,
A bit run-down and tired;

It was not thus in days of old
When gloomy lads and lasses
Lined up resignedly, come Spring
For sulphur and molasses.

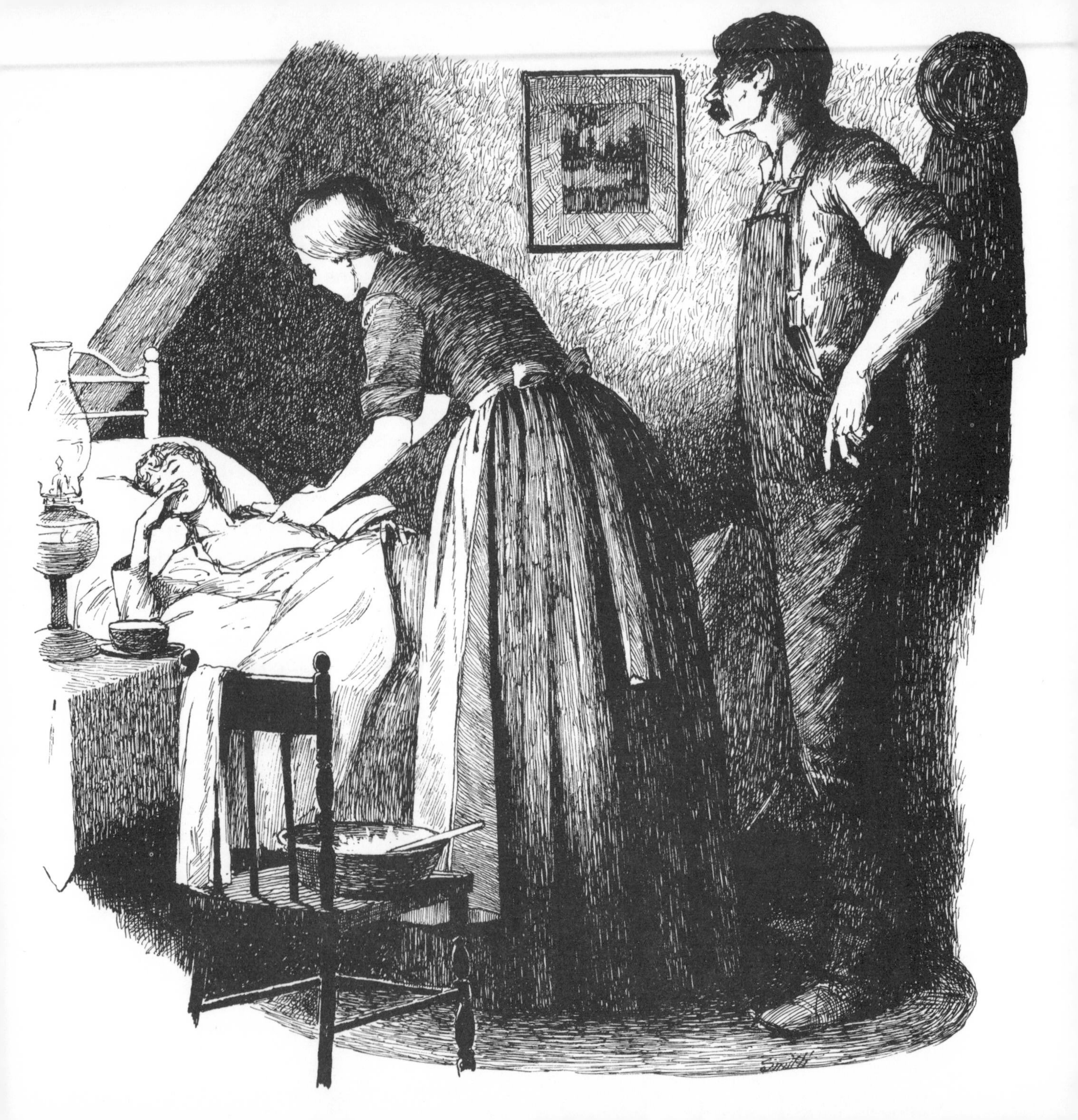
Smith

Poultices and Plasters

Sheep skin and beeswax
Make an awful plaster;
The more you try to pull it off
The more it sticks the faster.

- Old childhood chant

In the days of our grandparents and great grandparents, a surprising number of ills were treated with the miracle cures of poultices and plasters - concoctions of various healing substances applied to infected or aching parts of the body. The main difference between the two was that the ingredients of a plaster were generally stiff and paste-like, while those in a poultice were softer and more liquid. Although the two names were rather loosely used, some sources give very precise definitions of the two types of treatment. According to some, a plaster covered a larger area - usually the chest or back, and was used to treat breathing and lung problems. It was left on for a long time - over night or all day - and it required only body heat to make it "work". A poultice, on the other hand, was basically a bread or vegetable "magnet" for drawing out infection or foreign objects; it was changed often and the heat of each new application did as much to effect a cure as the actual ingredients did.

Whatever the differences, poultices and plasters did much to save life and limb. Perhaps their healing effects were as much psychological as physical, but there is no doubt that they often worked wonders. I recall an all-night vigil in my family's snowbound farmhouse, when a young man was suffering from blood poisoning, with red and blue streaks colouring his arm. Hot bread poultices, faithfully changed as they cooled, drew out the poison as patient and mother sat beside the wood stove while the blizzard raged outside.

Linseed, the seed of the flax plant, was a common ingredient for poultices. Both meal and oil were used. As a treatment for inflammation, linseed meal was mixed into a smooth paste with water, sandwiched between two pieces of soft cloth - usually flannel - and placed on the inflamed area. Linseed oil, mixed with epsom salts, was used as a poultice to draw out infection and remove slivers that had lodged under the skin. Boiled flaxseed, thickened with powdered charcoal, was considered a most effective poultice against gangrene.

Vegetables were also used for making poultices. Grated carrots or turnips were sometimes steamed and placed between layers of flannel, but onions were even more commonly used, perhaps because they were easily available at any time of the year. The onions were cooked until soft, stirred together with vinegar and linseed meal, and placed, as hot as could be borne, on the chest. This was a treatment for pleurisy or pneumonia. These common illnesses of pioneer days were also treated with onions cooked with goose fat and made into a savoury-smelling poultice. An elderly friend tells a story about two women who prepared such a poultice for a suffering member of their family. When the mixture was ready, they found the aroma so irresistible that they sat down and ate the whole preparation. The patient had to wait while they made another panful for external use - but undoubtedly the treatment was still effective!

Leaves of the toadflax plant, also called butter-and-eggs or wild snapdragon, were sometimes steamed and applied as a remedy for pulmonary infections. But perhaps the most common poultice of all in the days of home remedies was the familiar mustard plaster. Many people today can remember the stinging sensation and sharp smell of mustard applied to the chest to loosen a cough and attack a cold. An "old timer" has been defined as someone who can remember when the wonder drugs were mustard plasters and castor oil. More than one old-time physician habitually advised his patients, "When in doubt, apply a mustard plaster."

An elderly neighbour relates how, as a very young child, he became dangerously

ill with pneumonia. The doctor told his parents that he could do nothing more; the child was beyond help. But the family refused to accept the doctor's pronouncement and applied mustard plasters to the child's chest and back. By morning the crisis had passed and the boy was on the way to recovery. The doctor left the house to hurry down the road and prescribe the same treatment for another patient. She too recovered.

This miracle treatment was made with mustard mixed with flour, since mustard alone would be too harsh on the skin, especially for children. The mixture was moistened with warm water, placed between the usual pieces of soft cloth, and applied to the chest until it cooled, stiffened, and lost its power. When it was removed, an oil of some kind - usually goose oil - was gently rubbed into the chest to soothe the burning sensation on the skin. Some home nurses insisted that the oil be applied before the plaster, while others mixed it with the dry ingredients.

Turpentine and goose oil - again, an irritant and an emollient - provided another popular combination of ingredients for poultices; another favourite application for the treatment of colds and chest problems was a mixture of warm mutton tallow and partially melted beeswax, wrapped in a soft piece of sheepskin. The reasons for choosing various mixtures to treat certain ailments were not always clear. Perhaps their effectiveness often lay in the firm belief of both the patient and the home nurse that something was being done to ease the pain and discomfort.

In the days when wood was one of the most common materials of everyday living, slivers and splinters often found their way under the skin. These were very difficult to remove without proper instruments; left untreated, they could lead to inflammation, infection, and great pain. Hot poultices were the answer to this problem too. Steamed concoctions of such plants as pigweed, garden heliotrope, common wild thistles, nasturtium seeds, water lily roots, and burdock leaves were placed on the affected area. They were often helpful because the moist heat of the application actually softened the skin around the foreign object and drew it out, along with any infection that it might have caused.

Bread was a widely used material for poulticing an infected area. It was always on hand and was known to be effective, especially when a bit mouldy - the forerunner of penicillin. Rickett's blueing, a preparation designed to whiten clothing, and epsom salts were other ingredients sometimes used in the bread poultice; these were moistened with hot water or warmed sour milk. Another common ingredient for poultices was hops; a handful of hops was mixed in a cup of hot water and thickened with corn meal. It was believed that the yeast content of both the bread and the hops provided drawing power and literally pulled the infection out of the body. It was important, too, that a second hot poultice be held in reserve, to be applied as soon as the first one began to cool.

A paste made of soft yellow soap and brown sugar, moistened with hot water, was another popular concoction for drawing out infection and splinters. Oatmeal was also used as a basis for a soothing plaster; a Scottish physician described it simply as "porridge without salt" - and everyone knows the magical powers of porridge!

An effective agent for bringing a boil to a head was a split fig, secured over the painful area. This, it seems, has been used as a remedy since Old Testament times: "Let them take a lump of figs, and lay it for a plaister upon the boil and he shall recover." (Isaiah 38:21.) There does seem to be some scientific basis for this prescription; the acid of the fig cauterizes the wound while the heat ripens and draws out the infection.

Raw fat pork was the treatment of choice for carbuncles. A neighbour tells of once having a piece of pork, wrapped in soft flannel, placed on a troublesome carbuncle; it not only relieved the pressure and drew out the infection - it removed the entire core, leaving a hole the size of a pea in his foot. Apparently, as the pork heated from contact with the body, it would soon begin to "work".

Great Aunt Sally's receipt book - a fascinating compendium of folk lore that has been a treasure in our family for many years - recommends the application of salt pork rind over a puncture. In cases of swelling, the receipt suggests bathing the affected area with a strong wormwood decoction, followed by another pork treatment.

An old man who was a builder in his younger days describes how he once had his foot pierced with an old-time square nail. He tried treating the wound with a number of popular poultice ingredients, but nothing worked until he applied some gum from a fir tree. He was amazed to find that a fragment of wool from his sock, which had been forced through his flesh by the blunt end of the nail, was drawn out by the gum poultice. A similar claim was made for dried cattle manure, which heated up when applied as a poultice and drew out a bit of wool from a foot injury.

Several old friends and neighbours have provided me with detailed accounts of how dried or fresh cattle or sheep manure was used in poultices to draw out foreign objects and infection and promote healing. One woman recalls being sent to the sheep yard as a young child, to gather a supply of sheep manure which was then dried and set aside to be used for healing purposes whenever the occasion arose.

Cattle manure seems to have been a

prized poultice ingredient. I was told a story about a man whose doctor insisted that his leg must be amputated, after all efforts had failed to extract the infection from an old musket injury. Rather than allow this to happen, the patient's family decided to try poulticing the wound with fresh cow manure - and the leg was saved. Another story, told by a farmer over ninety years old, concerns a valuable colt with a stunted foot. A friend suggested that the farmer fill a bag with warm cow manure each morning and ease the colt's foot and lower leg into the soft, warm poultice bag. The farmer followed his friend's advice, and soon the foot and leg began to develop normally.

Another horseman tells a story about a horse which had a small stone embedded in the "frog" of its foot. The pebble was too deeply lodged to be removed, and the

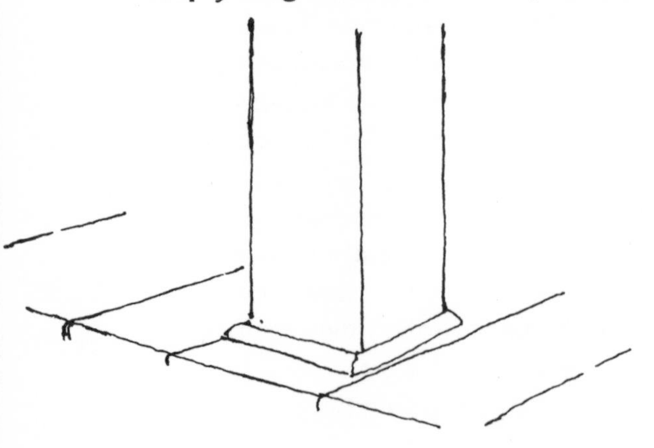

horse was unable to walk. It appeared that the animal would have to be destroyed, but the owner recalled hearing about the cow manure treatment and, as there was nothing to lose, he decided to try it. He changed the poultice often and tended the horse carefully. Amazingly enough, the pebble worked its way out through the upper surface of the hoof, against which it had been pressing. With the pressure relieved, the horse almost immediately began to limp about the yard, hesitatingly at first and then more briskly. In the days when horses were so important to the way of life of farm people, this must have been a cause for family rejoicing.

Smith.

Vanity, All is Vanity

The fair maid who, on the first of May
Goes to the woods at break of day
And bathes in the dew from the hawthorn tree
Will ever after handsome be.

- Old nursery rhyme

In earlier times, beauty aids as well as remedies had to be improvised from the materials at hand. Many of them came from plants found in the woods and clearings surrounding the homes. Herbs were widely used, both internally and externally, for health and beauty. Sage, for example, was credited with the prevention of, or cure for, almost every malady under the sun - it supposedly gave an assurance of everlasting health and beauty of both mind and body.

Women in our grandmothers' and great grandmothers' day felt that a pale complexion was the ultimate in beauty. It was also a sign of status and class: a "lady" whose skin was white obviously didn't have to toil in the fields or over a hot stove - or so it would appear. So even women who did have to work hard made every effort to appear as though their lives were elegant and free from care. Sunbonnets, wide-brimmed hats, and parasols shielded them from the ravages of the sun. Before going berry-picking or working in the garden or fields, the women would dust their faces generously with powder or flour as a preventative against sunburn or tan.

Freckles were also a source of embarrassment and worry, and women tried very hard to bleach them away. One prescription for getting rid of freckles was a mixture of one ounce of lemon juice, a quarter dram of powdered borax, and a half dram of dry white sugar. The concoction was allowed to stand for several days before use and then applied regularly. Another treatment for freckles involved a tablespoon of grated horseradish, stirred into a cup of buttermilk and set aside for a day before use. It can only be imagined that the perfume from this concoction did nothing to add to the allure of the lady who strove to attain the fragile look that was considered so desirable.

In the days when fireplaces were used for both heat and cooking, firescreens were important articles of home furnishing. Often built at home and decorated by the lady of the house in her scarce leisure hours, they were used to shield her from the tell-tale ruddiness caused by the heat of the fire. That, it was feared, would suggest that she had been toiling over an open fire - which, in fact, she probably had.

In later years, when high colour became fashionable, stylish women had to find ways to give their cheeks and lips the desired rosiness. The velvety leaves of the mullein plant, also called Quakers' rouge, were sometimes rubbed on the cheeks, as a stimulant, while wild strawberry and beet juice were used as lip and cheek cosmetics. Strawberries especially were highly prized and were used as both food and medicine as well as beauty aids. Extract of wild strawberry was prescribed as a remedy for mild diarrhoea, and the first strawberries of the season were held in such high esteem that they were carefully dried and reserved for the ill.

Prepared cosmetics gradually became available in pharmacies, but until fairly recently their obvious use was considered daring and not quite ladylike, so the simple, homemade preparations continued to be used. No doubt many women justified this use of artifice by telling themselves that simple household articles could not really be considered cosmetics.

Throughout history, stories have been told about elegant ladies bathing in milk to enhance their complexions. Milk was naturally far too valuable to our grandmothers and great grandmothers to be used in such an extravagant way, but they did use a little milk, often combined with yarrow, as a face mask. This was allowed to dry on the face; it acted as an astringent to banish wrinkles and soften the skin.

Face masks were also concocted from other foods found in the farm kitchen; egg white, oatmeal, honey, cucumber juice, and even crushed parsley were all common ingredients. The masks were left on for several hours and then carefully rinsed off to reveal - it was devoutly hoped - a new found beauty.

Rain water, collected in a barrel placed under the spout of the eave trough, was considered ideal for washing both skin and hair. As it fell through relatively unpolluted air, it was no doubt gentler and softer than today's rain water! Washing the face several times a day in pure rain water was believed to be effective in smoothing out wrinkles; one elderly woman I know who has a remarkable complexion says that she has never used anything but a "wash rag" and hot water on her face.

A great and very common blow to a woman's pride, in the days before cover-up cosmetics were available, was the pitted skin that often resulted from an attack of small pox. A simple preventive measure was used by many of the home nurses of the day; flour was generously dusted on the face of the patient when the pox first appeared and left on for the duration of the disease, with the eyes being carefully protected from both flour and light. This precaution did seem to lessen the chance of the patient being left with permanent ugly marks on the skin.

Although hair dye was considered not quite respectable until fairly recent times, women - and some men - who were vain enough to resent the arrival of the first grey hairs did indulge themselves in an attempt to hold back the passage of time. There were many receipts for hair colouring, and the aim, of course, was to hit on one that looked natural, so that this bit of vanity would pass undetected. One dye was made with crushed walnut shells or bark, with a little alcohol to preserve the potion, and a few cloves. It was allowed to age for a fortnight or so, with a daily shaking; a pinch of salt was then added to clarify the dye and it was carefully applied with a sponge or a piece of absorbent cloth.

An amazing receipt for a "gentleman's shampoo" called for half an ounce of carbonate of ammonia, dissolved with an ounce of borax in a quart of soft water; this was mixed with two ounces of glycerine in three quarts of Nova Scotia rum. The effects of this shampoo are only to be guessed at. Men with little hair no doubt used soft soap to shine their bald heads. Those who lived in hope of restoring their hair were advised to apply a parsley infusion or the juice of a raw onion to perform that miracle. I was told of one man who massaged his bald head with peeled leeks; the only result of this treatment was an irritated scalp.

An old Quebec receipt for hand lotion involved a mixture of slightly beaten egg yolk and glycerine, which was always stored in a cool dairy house or cellar.

Cleanliness and freshness were much more difficult to achieve in earlier days than they are now, but most people made a great effort to keep themselves and their surroundings as immaculate as possible. Many of the earlier homesteads were located near rivers, streams, or lakes whose waters had many uses for the settlers - not the least of which was bathing. One elderly woman declares, "Georgian Bay was our bath tub and every summer Saturday we were reminded of it." The problem was not so easily dealt with in the colder weather, when tubs of water for bathing had to be painstakingly carried and heated over the fire.

What couldn't be cleansed could sometimes be camouflaged; herbs and spices, as well as flowers from the garden and the woods, were used as deodorants and deodorizers. In public buildings, a good sniff of snuff was a temporary defence against the unpleasant odours that were commonplace. Nosegays, compact bouquets of highly fragrant blossoms, were presented to dignitaries at the beginning of their tours of institutions; the gesture was more than a gracious presentation - it was a necessity for those of delicate sensibilities.

Rose petals, often combined with spices and herbs as well as the petals from peonies or other fragrant flowers, were sprinkled on the earthen floors of the early cabins and under the cumbersome furniture that was fashionable in later homes. Some of the ornate heating stoves were constructed with special compartments for spices and petals; these would release their fragrance with the heat of the stove. Flowers were often dried for this purpose in the summertime and preserved for later use.

Some women, with little time or energy left over after the hard daily schedule that was their lot, tended to "let themselves go" and become dowdy matrons after

marriage. Some even justified this lack of concern for appearance and daintiness by suggesting that such preoccupations were frivolous. However, the more genteel women felt it was important to retain a certain dignity; by dint of careful manipulation of their precious time and family funds, they managed to clothe the family more or less in style and to take pride in their fastidiousness.

One woman told me about her grandmother, who subscribed to *Godey's Ladies' Book* in order to keep up with the fashions and foibles of the day. The preacher referred to her as a "very worldly woman" and many of the neighbours frowned on her frivolity. But it seems likely that envy was the reason for their ridicule - human nature hasn't changed that much in the last century!

The men were often not as concerned with cleanliness and appearance as the women - a fact that probably made the women's struggle for gentility even more difficult. Men slept in their underwear and in cold weather often left on their work shirts as well; by the end of the winter the atmosphere in the bedroom must have been less than delicate. Still, it was no doubt a matter of warmth and convenience, as the temperature in houses heated by wood stoves would drop to a chilling level on a cold winter's night, and the men would have to get up to stoke the fire long before dawn.

In the days before the arrival of electricity, the soft light of candles and, later, of oil lamps was probably the best beauty aid a woman could hope for. But it was not only the women who appeared to advantage in the magic glow of candlelight - it must have softened many glaring defects in the gentlemen also.

Enterprising merchants found a way to benefit from the interest of many people in matters of health and beauty; they sold or even gave away small looking glasses, or mirrors, with their nothing-less-than-magic health and beauty aids advertised on the back of each one.

It's little wonder that there were common sayings and proverbs which excused the flaws and unpolished appearance that the harsh light of day was certain to reveal. A less than beautiful woman could console herself with the idea that "beauty is only skin deep" and a man who was not as elegant as he might have been could always be thought of as a "diamond in the rough".

Smith.

Rheumatics and Remedies

For every evil under the sun
There is a remedy or there is none,
If there be one, seek to find it;
If there be none, never mind it.

- Old nursery rhyme

Listening to stories of earlier times in Canada, told by old men and women who have their own memories of the tales told by their parents and grandparents, one gathers that pain was stolidly accepted as a necessary part of life much more than it is today. Drugs and painkillers were not commonplace items, to be found at the pharmacy down the street; instead, household remedies, faith, and even superstition all played a part in dealing with the ills of the body.

Teeth - or the lack of them - caused much suffering to our ancestors, from infancy to senility. Preventive dental care was practically non-existent a hundred years ago and, in some homes, as late as fifty years ago. Tooth picks were sometimes used as cleaners; they were most often sharpened quills or "sprigs from the broom". When toothbrushes were used, there was often only one in the house, shared by the whole family.

Prepared dentifrices have long been available but they were not taken for granted as they are today. In homes where teeth were cleaned regularly, homemade cleansers were often used. Kitchen staples such as plain salt or soda were common dentifrices; a more exotic one was a mixture of soap and honey, blended in water and flavoured with rosewater or oil of wintergreen. Strawberry juice was considered an excellent tooth-cleanser and breath-freshener, and a preparation of honey and pulverized charcoal was said to ensure the proverbial teeth like pearls. Chewing burned toast was thought to be good for the teeth - this argument was no doubt often used to persuade family members not to waste toast that had had a bit too much fire.

People often endured excruciating pain that resulted from lack of tooth care, and untold misery was caused by pyorrhoea; it was said that either of these could drive the patient to distraction or extraction, and it's difficult to say which was the lesser of the two evils of the day. But there were many different home prescriptions that offered some relief from the pain. The simplest was to rinse the mouth again and again with a saline solution. A ginger poultice - ground ginger, sprinkled on a piece of hot flannel and dampened with hot vinegar - was sometimes bound around the face at bedtime. Diluted iodine was rubbed on aching gums to alleviate the pain. Throbbing nerves in diseased teeth could sometimes be stilled with lotion made from the tansy plant or oil of cloves, applied to a bit of absorbent cotton and packed into the cavity. Even a whole clove set into a cavity offered some relief.

When a toothache became unbearable there was no other solution but extraction; this operation was carried out without benefit of music, water coolers, saliva absorbers, or anaesthetic, and the "dentist" in early times was often the village blacksmith. One elderly man who has been a blacksmith all his life told me that it was often necessary for the smith to apply leverage by placing his knee on the shoulder of the patient while he pulled the tooth with special pliers. Women patients usually received somewhat more genteel treatment, but having a tooth pulled was still a traumatic experience and one that was naturally dreaded and put off as long as possible.

Teething infants were pacified by being given a rag to chew - usually the corner of a flannel blanket sweetened with a dab of honey or molasses. A strip of bacon rind was another common soother, given to the baby to ease the pain and help push the tooth through the surface of the gum. In severe cases, the gums were sometimes lanced, often with a common pen knife, although one old-time doctor admitted that the child often "objected strenuously" - and little wonder!

The first dentures were probably fashioned from wood, and were poor substitutes for the real thing. There are stories about ingenious makeshifts: a hunter in northern Ontario claimed to have used the teeth of his catch to enjoy barbecued venison, and from the Yukon comes a story about a toothless prospector who was said to have eaten bear steaks with the aid of the molars of the unfortunate bear. Perhaps these stories are apocryphal, as it's difficult to imagine just how these feats could be accomplished, but tall tales from earlier times have a certain appeal nevertheless.

An old expression common among rural people was used to indicate that they had little cash to spend: "nothing but the run of my teeth" apparently meant that they had plenty to eat but little else. When the teeth ceased to "run", they were seldom mended or replaced, so even eating became a major problem. False teeth have been available for a long time, but in earlier days they were beyond the financial means of most people and those who could afford them usually found them ill fitting.

An old man in my husband's family enjoyed good health and the use of most of his own teeth for more than ninety years, but in his middle years he had lost a few teeth and was persuaded to have himself fitted with a partial plate. But he found the ill-fitting denture a nuisance and, being an impulsive and impatient man, he several times decided that the thing was more trouble than it was worth and tossed it over a fence. Always, he was prevailed upon by his wife to search it out, usually with the help of the children.

But one fall, when the laden boughs of the wild apple trees proved too tempting, he removed his plate for the last time and tossed it into a freshly ploughed field. After all, how could a man enjoy a crisp, crunchy apple with such a miserable device in his mouth? This time, the plate could not be found; no doubt a pack rat or a crow had taken it off to its nest. As far as the old man was concerned, they were welcome to the "damnation dentures". So much for "store-boughten" teeth!

Tooth troubles were often indirectly connected with other health problems, ranging from indigestion - often simply a result of improper mastication of food - to rheumatic aches and pains, which were thought to be caused by infection from diseased teeth. Years of working outside in cold, wet weather and sleeping on damp mattresses in unheated bedrooms were probably more direct causes.

Some of the measures taken to ward off attacks of rheumatism were nothing less than superstitious: it is hard to imagine how a buzzard feather worn behind the ear could be an effective preventive, but there were people who put their faith in such magical notions. Application of liniment to aching joints seems to be a little more sensible, and many different concoctions were used for that purpose. A half ounce of camphor combined with three ounces of olive oil was one liniment which offered some hope of alleviating rheumatic pains. Other potions that were rubbed on affected areas were one part hartshorn in two parts sweet oil and an extract from the root of a poplar tree combined with dandelion wine or other spirits.

Mustard and turpentine, wormwood and thyme, and St. John's wort were all tried with some degree of success. The last two are rheumatic remedies of long standing; a commercial liniment still sold today contains a high percentage of wormwood and thymol, plus other ingredients.

Another old-time remedy which offered some relief from aches and pains was a combination of two Seidlitz powders - acid and alkaline powders wrapped separately in blue and white glassine papers. Mixed separately with water and then poured together, they effervesced and were to be drunk while still fizzing. Seidlitz powders, named after the healing mineral waters of Seidlitz in Bohemia, had a laxative effect and were considered the answer to many medical problems. Great care had to be taken to combine them as prescribed,and it was believed that dire things could happen if directions were not followed exactly. An old rhyming epitaph was a warning to the wise:

Here lies the body of Sara Ann Lowder
Who burst from drinking a Seidlitz powder;
Gone from this earth to her heavenly rest,
She should have waited till it effervesced!

There were several other home remedies for rheumatism, each of which had its partisans; again, it seems likely that the effectiveness of a remedy often depended on the faith of the patient and the home nurse. Parsley tea, consumed daily, was thought to be infallible by some people; others believed that nettles should be rubbed into the aching limbs as a counter-irritant. A bedtime bath for the affected areas, with very hot water drained from boiled potatoes, was another way of coping with the pain of rheumatism. Another "cure" was a combination of three ounces of coal oil with one ounce of skunk oil; this was warmed on a clean shovel, away from direct heat, and then rubbed into the aching joints. And, of course, there were those who swore that a medicinal tot of home brew eased the pain considerably.

An aged Maritimer claimed that a lasting cure for rheumatism, even in its crippling stages, could be had by bathing for half an hour each day in a tub of very hot water in which a cup of washing soda had been dissolved. Mustard baths were also thought to be soothing to stiff and aching joints and muscles.

Chronic rheumatism used to be taken almost for granted as an unavoidable aspect of the aging process, a "cross to be borne", but even it had some side benefits. It could be used as a perfectly legitimate excuse for sitting in the sun while others worked, and it also enabled its sufferers to develop some skill in weather forecasting - a certain kind of twinge in the joints was a sure indication that the weather was going to change for the worse. In most cases, the barometric change was no doubt matched with a similar change in the humour of the patient! Although the chronic rheumatism of old age had to be endured with little hope of real relief, there were a few methods of dealing with it which were sure to have some effect. Leeches, or blood suckers, were sometimes applied to the affected areas to draw out "diseased blood" and, for some people, this treatment was so distasteful that the mere mention of it would result in an affirmation that the pain was less severe. If all else failed, a good dose of castor oil could be administered, with an apple a day for good measure - a remedy that was precribed for all manner of ills.

One story I was told suggested that a sprint, performed under circumstances of extreme stress, was one of the surer - if temporary - cures for rheumatism. It seems that an elderly couple were both troubled with "the rheumatics", the woman more affected than her husband. They had tried all the remedies they knew of, and all that friends and neighbours could suggest, but nothing seemed to help. Finally they were told that if they could get to the cemetery at midnight, the atmosphere there would be eerie enough to effect a lasting cure. Although this treatment sounded even more far-fetched than some of the other useless cures they had taken, the old couple decided that there was nothing to be lost by giving this a try.

They bolstered their courage one night and set off for the graveyard, the old man laboriously carrying his wife on his back. By sheer coincidence, a pair of sheep rustlers happened to be plying their trade in a nearby clearing. As the man was about to ease his wife gently down onto a comfortable looking tombstone, one of the rustlers, considering a prospective victim, asked his partner in a hoarse stage whisper, "Is she *fat*?" The old man reacted wlth incredible speed. "Fat or lean, here she's to you!" he cried, dropping his helpless cargo and taking off through the woods for home. But, although he ran as fast as he could, he reached home to find his wife waiting on the doorstep for him, her cure having been even more powerful than his.

Smith

The Superstitious Way

In vain might midnight hags colleague
To witch poor Crumbie's milk, if she
Had only o'er her crib a twig
Cut from the rowan tree!

- Evan McColl, 1885

Throughout the history of the world, human beings have been superstitious; unexplained and unexplainable happenings have been accounted for with the telling of superstitious tales, and evil in its many guises has been warded off with superstitious rituals. It is in the nature of superstition that its origins have usually been lost in the mists of time, but it is clear that our ancestors brought their less-than-rational beliefs with them when they came to this country, so they cannot be labelled as specifically Canadian. And, for most of them, it is possible only to guess at the reasons why they developed and became popular.

The verse above gives a prescription for ensuring that a cow's milk would continue to flow in a sweet stream. In the days when a cow was a prized piece of property for most families, having her go prematurely dry was a problem to be avoided at all costs. One way of warding off this sad situation was to hang a branch of the rowan tree - usually called mountain ash in North America - above her stall; this was considered a guarantee that she would faithfully provide milk for the family. But wood from the rowan tree must not be used as fuel, for that would surely bring bad luck.

Ladders were considered lucky for lovers - but only if they were used for climbing up or down; it was bad luck to walk under them, and that belief persists today. Another superstition that still has many followers is that good luck resides in a four-leaf clover. But in earlier days it was believed that this only applied if the finder knelt down and bit the clover off with her teeth, rather than plucking it by hand.

A lover could be bewitched if a woman planted a sunflower seed in earth gathered from his footprint; as the plant grew and flourished, so would the love between the desired and the desiring. Another superstition had it that acquiring a taste for gooseberries would lead to a deepening of the affection between the gooseberry-eater and his or her beloved. Sharing a drinking vessel at a spring, pump, or open well was another way of intensifying a relationship; it was said that this tender act would inevitably lead to wedding bells.

Ferns were long considered to have magical powers, and Ben Jonson and Shakespeare both made reference to the ability of a concoction of fern seed to render its drinker invisible. It was also widely believed in earlier days that if a fern were touched by a person of less than admirable character, it would wither and die within a few hours. Another plant believed to have magical powers was the moonwort; if picked at the time of the full moon, it was supposed to have special characteristics.

Shoes, especially horseshoes, have always been objects of superstition; the most widely held belief was, of course, that a horseshoe, nailed open end up over a doorway, would trap good luck for the household. A complication of this superstition required that the shoe be secured with three nails; otherwise, luck would not be attracted to the home. This elaboration was passed on to me by an elderly blacksmith, who also pointed out that, for a smith to draw good luck to his forge, he must hang the horseshoe open end down. A seven-holed horseshoe was considered especially lucky, no doubt because of the mystical charm that has always been attached to the number seven.

For centuries, shoes have been tied to bridal vehicles and thrown after sailors to bring good luck. Squeaky shoes or boots were supposed to bring good fortune to an actor, although he might also be teased that they "complained" because they weren't paid for. According to some old-timers, cramps in the legs could be cured by turning one's shoes upside down beside the bed at night.

Sewing on the Sabbath used to be frowned upon, and it was said that every stitch put in with the hand on a Sunday would have to be removed with the nose on a Monday - in other words, breaking the taboo by sewing on Sunday would be worse than useless, because the work would not turn out well and would have to be ripped out and redone. It was also considered bad luck for a drop of blood from a needle-pricked finger to fall on a quilt; perhaps this too was more apt to happen if the quilt was worked upon on a Sunday.

"When I was a youngster, you dasn't whistle on a Sunday!" an over-eighty friend once exclaimed. Certainly, noise-making of any sort was looked upon as improper conduct for the Sabbath. An old saying had it that "A whistling girl and a crowing hen will always come to bad end" but, in the days when whistling was a lively form of entertainment, many girls and women were melodious whistlers and were often invited to amuse the guests at parties. As for the crowing hen, she probably ended up in the soup pot - but this must happen on a Friday or bad luck would surely befall the diners.

Birds were subjects of a number of superstitions and were often thought to have the power to influence people's destinies. An owl hooting near a house has long foretold ill fortune affecting that dwelling and the people who live there. It was said that if a heron somehow caused two people to meet, it would bring a strange mixture of happiness and sorrow into their lives. A bird fluttering around a window has often been considered a sign of death; I myself have received a call announcing a death in the family even as I watched a bird frantically battering its wings against a window of my house.

A howling dog has also been taken to be a death sign and one older woman told about a strange dog suddenly appearing on her doorstep, not howling but actually crying; within a very short time, her husband passed away.

Since time immemorial, cats have been regarded as creatures of mystery, perhaps because they seem so independent and move so silently. Black cats have often been considered unlucky, especially to those whose paths they cross. Theatre people, however, have traditionally thought that a cat of any colour should be given free access to the stage, as it would bring good fortune to the performance.

Three-coloured cats have a special place in superstitious lore; true tortoiseshell cats are invariably female and so a male tortoiseshell, if one could be found, would be a special, lucky animal. It is said that Queen Victoria once offered a fifty-pound reward for anyone who could bring her a male tortoiseshell cat; the reward was never claimed. Scientists would now tell us that the reason for this has something to do with X chromosomes; male tortoiseshells do in fact exist but are seldom capable of reproducing, so they are of course extremely rare.

There are a number of well-worn superstitions about snakes. Serpents have long been believed to be immune to infection and it is no doubt for that reason that the snake became a symbol for the medical profession. Repulsive to many people, snakes, harmless or not, have often been killed indiscriminately; however, an old belief insisted that a dead snake should be turned right side up to prevent a devastating rainstorm.

Snakes moving sluggishly in summer were believed to foretell a lean harvest in the fall, and this notion seems to have had a sound basis in fact. Snakes prey on rodents, so sluggish snakes are probably full snakes, which would in turn signal the presence of a greater than usual number of rodents in the fields. If the rodents weren't kept down by the snakes, they would eat more of the grain, and that would naturally lead to a smaller than normal harvest.

As bread has always been thought of as the staff of life and salt as the spice of life, it is not surprising that these two items have traditionally been given to people moving into a new home. The double housewarming gift brought with it a wish that food would always be plentiful in that home. Scottish people believed that it was tempting fate to bring salt from an old home to a new one, so this notion too may have influenced the selection of gifts. Salt was scarce and valuable during the early days in this country and it was believed to be very bad luck to spill any. But it is hard to imagine why throwing a pinch of the precious commodity over the left shoulder, thus wasting more of it, would change the luck from bad to good!

According to a salt manufacturer, the old-time buffalo stampedes did not happen because the animals were in search of more lush feeding grounds but because they were driven by an insatiable salt hunger; they would leave pleasant pasture grounds only to go on the rampage for a new salt supply.

An old superstition claimed that "You have to eat a peck of dirt before you die!" Given the sanitary conditions of the day, there was probably a good deal of truth in the comment.

Rural people habitually shook the tablecloth out the door after a meal, tossing the crumbs to the chickens and birds. But some people believed that to do this after darkness fell would be tempting fate. Perhaps this was because it might then attract nocturnal nibblers such as mice, which were never welcome around the farmhouse.

Another popular superstition had it that accepting a slice of bread or a pat of butter when you still had some on your plate would be sure to bring a hungry person to your door. To have a "hole in the bread plate" - that is, to let the bread tray become empty, especially if guests were present - was unlucky too. Certainly it was considered a breach of hospitality and a source of great embarrassment to the homemaker.

"Strange little happenings" were said to

befall anyone who stirred tea or coffee with anything but a spoon, but it was a common practice for people to pour the hot beverage into a deep saucer and sip from it rather than drink from the cup.

Another common superstition, often repeated to youngsters, threatened, "Sing before you eat, cry before you sleep." Perhaps this was simply another warning that children were expected to be seen and not heard when adults were around, and singing was considered even more of an intrusion than speaking.

In the days when families were larger than they are today - families of twenty-four children were not unheard of - "the seventh son of a seventh son" was believed to be endowed with strange powers. A child whose father died before the infant's birth was thought to have a special ability to charm away disease and turn ill fortune into good; perhaps this was his compensation for having to grow up without the benefit of paternal love and wisdom.

A baby who was born enveloped in a caul, or membrane, was thought to be forever safe against death by drowning, and a superstitious sailor would gratefully receive the caul of such a child and carry it always on his person, to protect him from a watery grave.

Children born during extreme climatic events - meteors, northern lights, electrical storms, and so on - were believed to be destined to live uncommon lives, and desperately ill people, in the short time before they died, were thought to be endowed with special prophetic gifts.

The old saying, "Dream of the dead, lose one of the livlng" was widely taken with great seriousness. It was also a common belief that if a patient, in his delirium, spoke of the dead, he would soon join them. One old man in my husband's family, who had been an ardent horseman, began to shout loudly and at length from his sick bed to a favourite team of horses who had long been dead. For days, according to the family, he "drove" that team before he finally, in utter exhaustion of mind and body, "lay down the reins" and passed on, perhaps to join them in another world.

Another old saying, "A green Christmas, a fat churchyard" - that is, a full graveyard - may also have had some basis in fact, as a winter with little snow was usually one with a great deal of damp, unhealthy weather, which was highly dangerous for bronchial sufferers and the like.

At funerals, care was taken to try to avoid a noticeable gap in the procession of vehicles, because that was a sign of another funeral in the near future. When a candle or kerosene lamp blew out of its own accord, that too was taken as an omen signifying the death of an acquaintance or friend. Even in the early days of electricity, there were people who took the burning out of a street lamp as the signal for an upcoming death.

As might be expected, there were many superstitions about ghosts and spirits in the early days. One belief had it that it was possible to communicate with spirits but not with ghosts - the difference between them apparently being that spirits could not be seen but could talk, while ghosts could be seen but would not speak. It was also widely believed that midnight was the hour of witches and two a.m. was the hour of demons. Another old adage claimed that if you used an individual badly during his lifetime, his spirit would come back to haunt you after death.

Inanimate objects were often credited with supernatural powers; rocking chairs in abandoned houses were chief among these, and there were tales of such rocking chairs moving of their own accord. This could perhaps be simply explained by the fact that the rockers were so well balanced that the slightest tremor or breeze would cause them to rock gently, giving the effect of some unseen force at work.

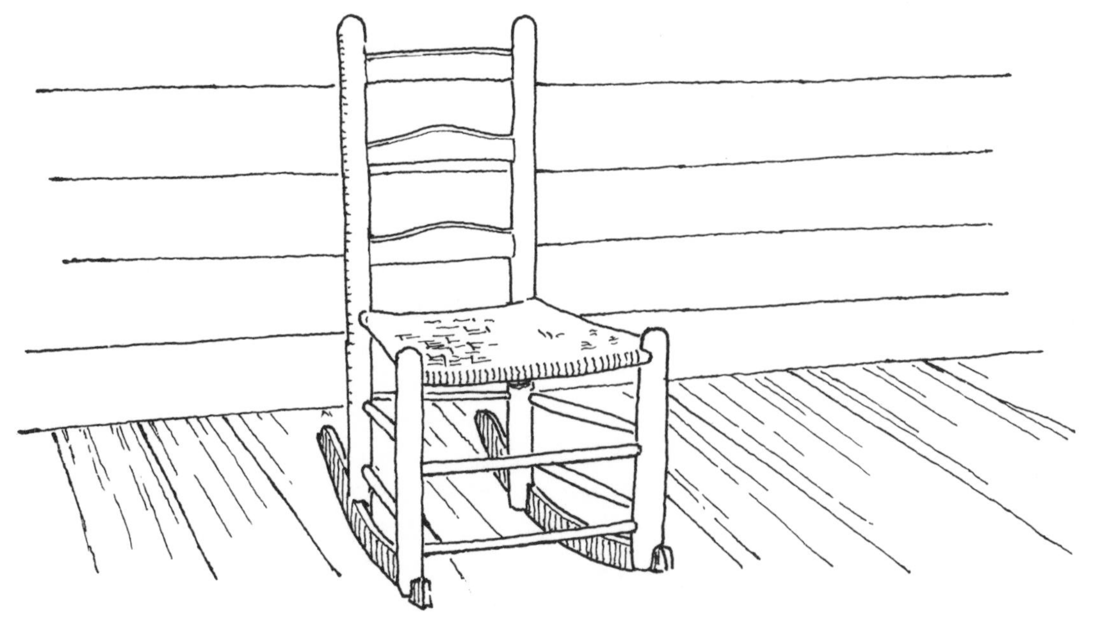

An elderly woman told of having won a piano in her younger years, not through purchase of a lucky ticket, but by dint of her own hard work. She had sold subscriptions to a rural newspaper, walking many miles in isolated areas and travelling by train, and had been so successful that her industry was rewarded with the gift of a piano. A popular superstition said that it was bad luck to sell anything that had been won, so she kept the piano until, in her later years, she was obliged to move into smaller quarters; she then gave it to her niece, with the stipulation that it should never be sold.

Another woman, who professed to be an authority on spirits and ghosts, told of a piano in a lovely old home in Montreal. This piano must have been won and then sold, for it rebelled against being played. Anyone who dared to try to play it immediately froze to the seat of the piano bench and broke out into a cold sweat. Every night, footsteps could be heard on the verandah of the house, walking back and forth, back and forth - although the light of morning revealed no footprints, even on freshly fallen snow.

Inadvertently placing a chair in front of another was taken as a signal that fascinating visitors were sure to present themselves at your door. Silverware was also thought to have some bearing on the family's social life: a dropped spoon meant that a child would visit, a fork would bring a woman caller, and a knife a gentleman visitor.

Brooms were considered to have a touch of the supernatural about them; for some reason it was said that when people moved from one house to another they should never take a cat or a broom with them. It was also thought to be dangerous to sweep with a broom after dark, because that would disturb the household spirits. People believed that a witch could never cross over a broom; if a broom placed across a doorway had mysteriously moved during the night, it was a sure sign that a witch had passed through the house.

In western Canada it was believed to be bad luck to accept a two-dollar bill. This superstition probably had its origin in the fact that, in the gambling houses of the wild west, turning up a "deuce" in a card game meant that the player would have little gain.

In the days when gypsy caravans travelled throughout the country, people were warned never to forget a debt to a gypsy, for they were thought to be endowed with magical powers and would surely retaliate if they were treated badly. Most people were sure that gypsies were clairvoyant, and their fortune-telling skills were taken very seriously. In palm reading it was said that the right hand told about what you were born with and the left hand indicated what you had made of your life, your character, and your health. It was considered to be very bad luck to attempt to tell your own fortune.

Many of the gypsy fortune tellers were known to be adept at picking pockets, and a story is told about a young couple who made their living this way. In time they were awaiting the birth of a little pick-pocket, and they talked about how, with the early training they would give their child, he or she would ensure that in a very few years their fortune would be made. A midwife was brought in for the delivery and a healthy child was brought into the world. But the baby was born with a clenched fist - a sure sign that he would grow up to be "careful with money". But how could a clenched fist pick pockets effectively?

Try as they might, the infant could not be induced to unclasp his hand. In desperation, the parents called in a wise old doctor and, with some embarrassment, shared their problem with him. The doctor took out his gold pocket watch and held it out to the child. As the tiny fist snapped open to grasp it, from the open palm fell the wedding band of the midwife.

Bugs and Beasties

Good night, sleep tight, don't let the bugs bite
If they bite, squeeze them tight
And they'll not bite another night.

- Old childhood chant

Perhaps the most common "wee beasties" that the farmers of earlier days had to contend with were field mice; they damaged the crops in summer and they could always find holes big enough to squeeze into the barns and houses for winter shelter and board. Many devices were used to trap or otherwise discourage the little creatures, which were a constant problem - as they remain today. Every farm had at least one cat and often several; and people used to say that nothing would keep mice down like a cat with kittens, and there was usually one around. But cats were seldom allowed in the house. Many people believed that "A cat will take a baby's breath away", so the cats usually exercised their mouse-hunting abilities in the barn rather than the house.

Another mouse chaser, guaranteed to equal any cat, was a mixture prescribed by a chatelaine in a pioneer village in Quebec: a pound of pulverized red pepper, mixed with flour and a bit of corn starch, and packed into mouse holes and crevices. Some people even plugged up their entrances with prickly green burrs from the burdock plant, presumably with the hope that the nose of a mouse, like that of a bear, is his most vulnerable spot.

Weasels and ferrets also spelled disaster to mice. Weasels were often found around farm buildings and, in spite of their mouse-hunting abilities, were looked upon with distaste by many people. It took a certain amount of coolness to accept a family of weasels taking up residence in the back kitchen, which was not used in the winter, but there were some people who saw them more as pets than pests - at least as long as the mouse population was kept down.

Next to mice, flies were the greatest plague on the farms of days gone by; fighting them was a never-ending battle in spring, summer, and fall. Until more scientific fly-killers came along, the homemakers concocted lethal mixtures from common household substances; these were usually placed in shallow dishes and set out of reach of children and pets, in the hopes of tempting the flies away from the cooking and dining areas.

A favourite method of clearing flies from a room before a meal was to set out a mixture of equal amounts of brown sugar and black pepper, dampened with milk. Another effective potion was the poisonous juice of the toadflax plant, mixed with milk, which attracted the flies; this concoction also had to be kept out of reach of children.

The old saying, "You can catch more flies with honey than with vinegar," holds a measure of literal as well as figurative truth. Even plain molasses in a shallow saucer or pie plate ended the flight of countless flies in many homes. An old home almanac prescribed water taken from boiled onions as a cleaner for windows and looking glasses; it was said to prevent the glass from being sullied with fly-specks. The scent of geraniums was also considered a powerful deterrent against flies entering a room, so it is no wonder that most farm kitchens had rows of the brightly coloured flowers along their window ledges.

So persistent was the fly problem, especially at preserving and pickling time, that a stirring spoon was often slipped through a slit cut in a piece of cloth which was used as a pot cover, saving the sweet-smelling, bubbling jams and relishes from acquiring an unwanted protein content.

To keep flies from entering the inner rooms of the home, doors were left closed and blinds or heavy drapes were drawn most of the time; this also helped to keep the house cool in the days when, even in summer, a wood fire was used for cooking.

If they could be kept confined to the kitchen, flies could be dealt with much more easily, and they were often "herded out" the door before a meal. Armed with aprons, towels, or other pieces of cloth, family members would each choose a corner of the room and then converge on the flies, swishing them out of the corners and shooing them through the open door. Strips of newspaper, secured to a long stick, were also ideal for this purpose; they were used in my family's home each day during the fly season.

Herbs such as wormwood, tansy, and mint were hung from the rafters of homes and barns to discourage flies. Soapy water from the laundry or housecleaning was often left sitting in the kitchen for an hour or so, to catch a few flies before being thrown out the door. Window and door screens made from cheesecloth, and later wire, were no proof against the crafty flies which would hover near the doorways, ready to flit into the house whenever a member of the family went in or out.

Eventually, commercial "fly pads" became available from the general store or from the pedlars who, in diminishing numbers, still called on homes in isolated areas. These dried pads were dampened and set in strategic places to trap flies. The later sticky fly coils, hung from kitchen ceilings, were as successful at "catching" people's hair as they walked by as they were at dealing death to flies. And, of course, when all else failed, the buzzing flies could always be assaulted with fly swatters.

Coal oil lamps, with their tall chimneys, were lures for both flies and moths, which were attracted by the flickering light to meet their doom in the flames. Moths were a particular menace in the days before synthetic fabrics, when most clothing and blankets were made of wool; fighting them demanded the housewife's energy and ingenuity. Spices were effective against moths and have been used for centuries, and citron is known to have been used by the early Romans to get rid of the troublesome creatures. Our grandmothers and great grandmothers also used marking chalk from the sewing basket to deal with ants; they marked the path of the ants with the chalk and the ants simply disappeared - or found another route. Cucumber peelings, walnut leaves, salt, cloves, cedar, camphor, and pepper were all used as repellents against moths, ants, and other insects.

An old cousin of my family was a gardener of note and swore by his insect powder, which he used against all manner of creeping and crawling creatures that might attack his plants. Hughie's insect powder consisted of one pint of crude carbolic acid, three pints of gasoline, and fourteen pounds of plaster of Paris, carefully combined and spread on heavy brown, absorbent paper to allow the gasoline to evaporate. It was then stored in a can or box with a tight-fitting lid, out of reach of children and pets. Dusted onto garden plants and rubbed through screens of windows and doors, this mixture really did seem to be effective against insect marauders.

The old chant at the head of this chapter was often shouted by children - sometimes much to the chagrin of their parents. Most of the youngsters, according to an elderly teacher, didn't have any idea of what bedbugs were like, but a chant has always been irresistible to children. In some homes, bedbugs really were a problem, and overnight guests sometimes introduced that particular nuisance to a household. In the days when distances seemed longer and transportation was much more difficult, families were often obliged to put up travellers whose cleanliness might be questionable. One such guest in our household was an old quack "horse doctor", whose own horse expired while walking up our lane, despite - or perhaps because of - its owner's medicine.

On the day after such an overnight visit, the bedclothing would have to be washed separately from the family laundry and the bedposts and the crevices along the baseboards were wiped with a rag soaked with coal oil - just in case. As children we were told that our grandmother would have dipped a goose wing into a strong solution of alum and painted along any cracks or corners in a room where a pedlar or itinerant had spent the night. As the family lived on the main road to Ottawa, there were many such travellers in the early days.

My grandparents' family boasted seven stalwart sons and, when the farm work slackened off in the fall, some of them "went to the shanty" - that is, to work in the lumber camps further up the Ottawa Valley. In those days, when sanitary conditions were much more difficult to achieve, especially in places like lumber camps, my grandmother would not allow the boys to return directly home in the spring when their winter work was over. They were expected to get a room with bath in Ottawa, discard their shanty clothes completely, scrub themselves clean, and return home in newly purchased and respectable attire.

In recent years, when it has become fashionable to renovate century-old homes, new owners have often stripped off the layers and layers of wallpaper applied over the life of such a home. Between these layers, bedbugs have sometimes been found, having feasted for generations upon the dried flour-and-water paste.

A century-old receipt for a bedbug remedy sounds quite convincing, since it claims that "If it is put on a bedbug he will never step afterward, and if put into crevices it will destroy their eggs and thus drive them from the premises." The concoction consisted of two ounces of aqua ammonia, one quart of soft water, one teaspoon of saltpetre, and one ounce of shaving soap or one three-cent cake, finely shaved or scraped. This was mixed well together and shaken vigorously, then allowed to stand for a few hours to give the soap a chance to dissolve before being used. As an added bonus, this mixture was supposed to be effective in removing greasy fingerprints from doors and woodwork; other claims were that it would shampoo like a charm and would not harm the finest fabrics.

One woman who was an innkeeper solved the bedbug problem by periodically closing all windows and doors and burning five pounds of sulphur in an old pot, set within a pail or tub with a few inches of ashes or sand in the bottom. This was claimed also to be a sure killer of flies, lice, ants, spiders, moths, and everything else that flew, hopped or crawled. Of course, since the fumes of sulphur are poisonous to all living things, people and pets had to be protected from it as well, so using this cure was a complicated procedure.

A simpler solution was to use a mixture of water and epsom salts which, while perhaps not as effective, did not require the upsetting of household activities. In desperation, in a pest-ridden home, a bedbug was sometimes placed in a coffin with a corpse, in the belief that the remaining bugs would vacate the premises when the coffin was carried out.

During the Depression years, when most people were forced to become even more enterprising, a "sure bug killer" was advertised in many rural papers. It was described as being simple and effective, and was available by mail for only twenty-five cents. Although money was scarce, this did not seem to be a great price to pay for something that would really take care of the potato bug problem, and many people sent off a quarter and waited for the return mail with great anticipation. In a few days, a package would arrive and would be eagerly opened. Out of it came a cube of wood and a small wooden mallet, as well as explicit instructions. On the wood block was printed, "Set them on this," and on the mallet, "Hit them with this."

A sense of humour was as important as the twenty-five cents in those days, and the block and mallet became a conversation piece in many homes. However, the potato growers still had to deal with the bugs that plagued their crops. One way of doing this was to sprinkle Paris green through cheesecloth onto the potato foliage, either very early in the morning when the dew was still on the plants or following a rain. Most people with small potato patches simply picked the bugs off the plants by hand - a task that was often given to the children of the family. One older person told me how she and her brothers and sisters had found that a goose wing made a perfect "swisher" for knocking off the bugs and, especially, the repulsive larvae which they did not want to touch.

The bugs were then dropped into a can, often with a bit of coal oil in the bottom, which would kill them on contact. Otherwise, they could be put into a dry can with a lid and later fed to the hens, who would gobble them up eagerly. This seemed a more practical method; although the word "recycle" had not entered the common vocabulary, it was commonly practised from pioneer days right through the Depression years.

Since the early days, farmers have believed that a few flax seeds sprinkled in each potato hill at planting time would discourage the potato beetle; another common practice was to plant potatoes under a mulch of straw, which was said to ensure a bug-free potato patch.

Fleas were more common in days gone by than they are now, and they sometimes transferred their affections from animals to people, causing itching and inflammation. Salt, sprinkled on the coat of a cat or dog, was said to banish the fleas quickly; for their human victims, the answer to the problem was simply a good scrubbing. However, fleas had another role to play: a flea circus was a popular form of entertainment, and the little creatures could be trained to perform tricks - they hopped, skipped, and jumped in a lively way. For a young lad or a bored bush camper, losing a trained flea to an old hound dog was nothing short of a catastrophe.

Snakes, too, elicited mixed feelings in earlier days. They were good mousers, but they also devoured toads and frogs, which were insect eaters and good for the soil; they were even known to eat chickens and birds, as well as eggs. I once saw a snake swallow a frog and, before it could slither away to digest its meal, my brother caught it and carefully eased the frog back out of the snake's mouth with his foot - and we watched fascinated while it hopped away. Snakes sometimes found their way into damp stone basements where they would help themselves not only to mice but also to pans of milk or other delicacies which had been set out to cool on the stone shelves.

Rattlesnakes were once quite common in some parts of Canada and they were a real concern, as a snake bite could be fatal, especially to children. It was believed that if you killed a poisonous snake you must immediately search out and kill its mate, which would be sure to be somewhere near by. This belief had some truth in it, but only during mating season.

It was important that a snake bite be treated immediately, before the venom reached the bloodstream. The wound was often cut or burned out, and sometimes the venom was even sucked out if there were no mouth wounds. Another treatment for snake bite was green horehound, an herb with bitter, aromatic juice. The juice was sometimes taken internally, or the foliage of the plant was made into a poultice and applied to the wound. Thoroughwort was used in much the same way, and a mixture of salt and raw egg yolk was another prescription for snake bite. A little alum mixed with water could be drunk, and juniper berries could be chewed as a counter-poison.

Some of the recommended cures for snake bite were as dangerous as the bite itself; the old saying, "Take a bite of the dog that bit you," was applicable to one remedy which was advocated. It was suggested that the victim kill the poisonous snake, cut it into pieces, and bind them on the wound; it was thought that this would extract the poison in a very short time. If the victim had the presence of mind and the wherewithal, he could immediately apply a tourniquet to prevent the poison from spreading and then place a poultice, made from whatever was available, on the wound; this, it was hoped, would draw out the poison.

As a child I was told a story about a woman in an isolated area who was bitten by a poisonous snake when she was alone at the farm with her small children. She was sure that the bite would kill her, and her only thought was to prepare enough food to keep her children alive until their father's return. She worked long and hard, baking bread over a hot fire and cooking soups and stews, and - much to her amazement - the poison was thrown off in her profuse perspiration. Whether the story was fact or fiction, it offered a strong moral about the virtues of unselfishness.

Although domestic bees were quite rare in pioneer days, people who wanted honey could get it - albeit with some risk. Wild bees were often tracked to their hives, high up in the trees, and a single bee could lead an observant person to a store of delicious honey that could be taken by the adventurous. Bears could scent honey easily, so a well clawed tree trunk was often a sign of honey further up. The claw marks on the tree did not necessarily mean that the honey was gone, because the bear's attempts to find himself a feast were often frustrated by the bees' angry reaction - his nose was especially vulnerable to their stings. People on the lookout for honey took more precautions than the bears did, but for them, too, honey-hunting expeditions could be rather painful. Woodsmen often chopped down a bee tree, sometimes by accident and sometimes after months of careful watching. If this was done after the storehouse of the bees was filled in the fall and the honeymakers were in their drowsy winter state, it was possible to gather a good-sized pail of honey without too much danger.

However, bee stings were always a problem and the pioneers often applied wet mud for relief, following the example of the bears. Dampened baking soda, clothes blueing, and herbs such as tarragon or savoury were also used in poultices to draw out the sting and ease the pain inflicted by angry bees. The stinging nettle plant was sometimes used as a counter-irritant against the stings of wasps or bees, and the juice of the milkweed was considered an effective treatment by some people. One elderly Maritimer told of being ferociously attacked by a whole swarm of bees one day when he was haying; the country doctor prescribed the juice of chewing tobacco as the simplest, handiest, and cheapest relief from the pain of the bee stings. According to the farmer, the treatment worked wonders.

A series of couplets about the swarming of bees was passed down as traditional knowledge from one generation to another: "A swarm of bees in May/ Is worth a load of hay. A swarm of bees in June/ Is worth a silver spoon. A swarm of bees in July/ Isn't worth a fly!" There was some truth in this judgment: if bees were swarming in July, they would not have enough time to establish a new hive and gather a good store of pollen before frost set in.

Horses were sometimes victims of bee stings - especially white horses, for it is said that bees are particularly attracted to white. On more than one occasion, a horse was killed by bee stings; as horses and bees are both inclined to be nervous creatures, the first sting would "spook" a horse and his reaction would bring down the whole swarm upon him. Many years ago, a remedy for bee stings appeared in a rural newspaper and was later reprinted in a nature magazine; it was described as a remedy for horses, but perhaps could have served as a treatment for human sufferers of bee stings. The remedy called for dipping blankets in a brine made from ten pounds of salt in a boiler of water as hot as the hands could endure; the blankets were then wrung out and wrapped around the tormented animal. This treatment was guaranteed to offer instant relief, and a complete cure within two hours.

The common leech or blood-sucker was another creature that was looked upon with a mixture of respect and distaste in earlier times. Bloodletting has been practised for centuries as a treatment for too thick or diseased blood - which was considered a cause of many ailments and symptoms. Doctors might sometimes use a lancet to release the blood but, more often, leeches were placed on the patient's flesh to obtain the desired result. The leeches sometimes had to be encouraged to do their job, perhaps with an appetizer of a film of milk wiped on the skin. It was also believed that their appetite could be heightened by allowing them to crawl on a dry, rough cloth before being placed on the victim. As many as forty leeches were sometimes applied at a time - it is little wonder that nightmares were also a common problem.

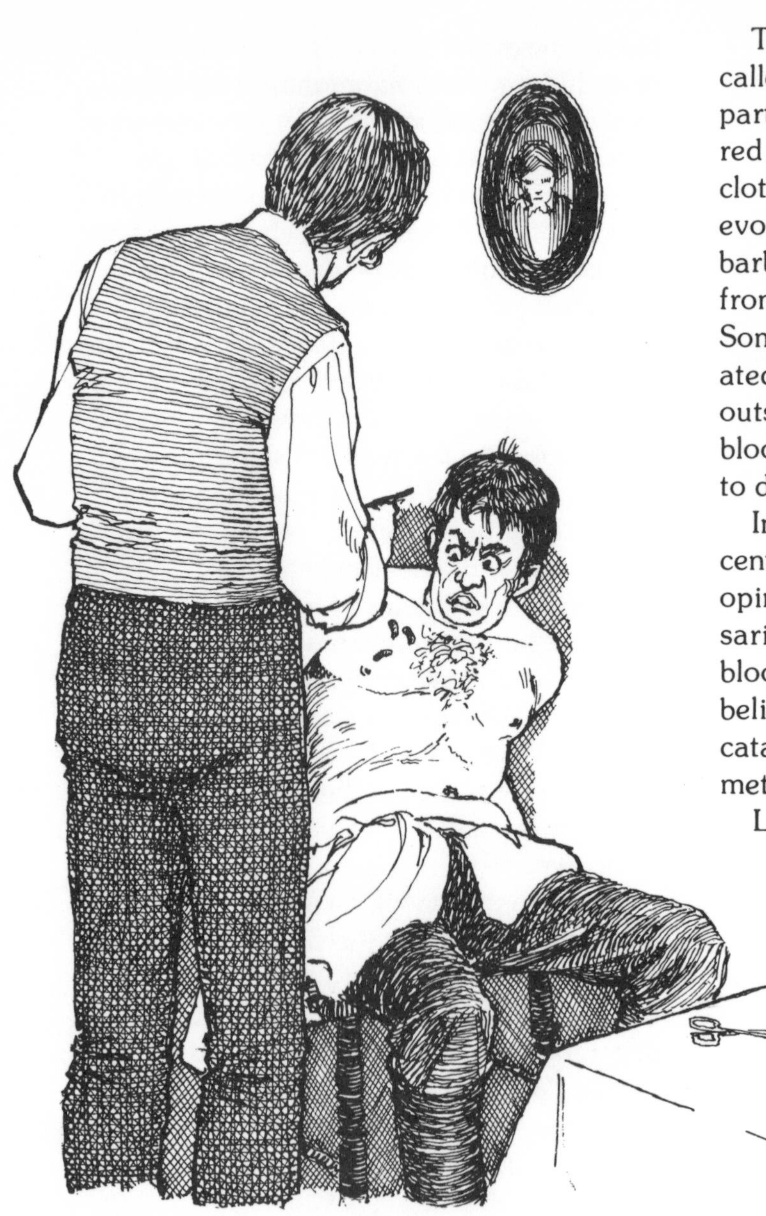

The old-time barber-surgeons were often called leeches because bloodletting was part of their practice. Their symbol was a red pole with a bowl and a strip of white cloth dangling from it; this sign later evolved into the red-and-white striped barber pole which was commonly seen in front of barber shops until recent years. Some old-timers claim that the sign originated with a practical horizontal pole outside the leech's shop, over which the blood-streaked white bandages were hung to dry.

In the latter part of the nineteenth century, a doctor-author expressed the opinion that people were dying unnecessarily because the grand old remedy of bloodletting had fallen into disuse. He believed that "half the complaints in the catalogue" would have been cured by this method in earlier days.

Leeches were sometimes applied to

inflamed areas caused by stings of bees or wasps - perhaps a case of the cure seeming worse than the ailment. The leeches had to be watched carefully, for when they had sated themselves on the inflamed area they would often move to a fresh meal on another part of the body. A pinch of salt would force them to release their tenacious hold; they would then be placed in a jar of water, with a coarse linen cloth securing the top, until their services were called for again.

An old quack doctor claimed that any old nag could be rejuvenated into a race horse by bloodletting. If the success stories about the leech treatment were all true, it is strange indeed that the practice is not still in use today.

Smith

From Horse to Horseless Carriage

An automobile of the latest design
Its use I will never disparage,
But for comfort and pleasure, pray give me for mine
A McLaughlin reliable carriage.

- Robert McLaughlin, 1905

From the days of the earliest settlements in this country, getting from one place to another has been a major preoccupation. Horses were highly prized, not only for their capacity for work - clearing the land, ploughing, tilling, and harvesting - but also because for years they provided a major means of transportation. The lakes and rivers of the country were of course very important routes from one place to another, but for land travel the horse had no peer. Oxen could pull heavier loads than horses, but they moved much more slowly. Early in the eighteenth century a number of brood mares and a stallion were sent out to Quebec by the King of France. A stiff fine was to be imposed on anyone who allowed a horse to die prematurely - although how this could be determined is not clear. For some time horses remained rare and precious in the eastern settlements; only the gentry could afford to own them, and in any case, oxen were considered better suited to the rough work of clearing the land. There are stories about wild herds of horses roaming the western plains, and the Plains Indians are believed to have ridden horses while they were still uncommon in Lower Canada.

Horses gradually replaced oxen on

Canadian farms and they were seen as prized and valuable possessions. A mare in foal was especially treasured and was spared from heavy work such as pulling stumps or dragging logs over rough trails. However, farmers believed that if a mare was lightly worked until the very hour of foaling, her offspring would be strong and healthy - and would thus add to her owner's property and prestige. The most practical time for a foal to arrive was between the middle of May and the middle of June; the mare could then be used in the lighter work of cropping before the birth and would be ready for heavier work by harvest time.

The arrival of a new colt or filly ranked second only to the birth of a child in the family. When wax formed on the teats of an expectant mare, announcing that the birth was imminent, there was great excitement in the farm family - and, indeed, there still is. It has always been a thrilling experience to watch a mare spring to her feet after giving birth and tear away the membrane from her offspring with her bared teeth. Farmers have always believed that there was less risk of problems if the birth occurred on a high, clean, grassy knoll rather than in a stable or barnyard.

It was not unusual to see a mare working in the fields with her foal running by her side. Many people were convinced that if a foal were weaned at the proper phase of the moon, there would be no fuss from mare or foal; they also believed that there was a right time in the lunar cycle for neutering a young colt.

Another strongly held belief was that if a donkey were allowed to run with horses, the horses would be immune to disease, just as goats with a herd of cattle were thought to give insurance against bovine tuberculosis or contagious abortion.

Horses have definite personalities, and in the days when horse and owner were obliged to work together in all kinds of weather and in many difficult situations, it was important for the owner to build a strong rapport with his horse and to understand the particular quirks of the animal. Some horses would work equally well for any person, but there were many who would be as gentle as a kitten with one driver and then absolutely refuse to co-operate with another driver. One old-time horseman tells of horses that would "tear up hell by the acre" if new owners dared to harness them.

Before the middle of the nineteenth century, agricultural fairs became important events in the lives of the rural folk. These were designed to encourage improvement in farm stock and produce from field and farm, and they were also looked upon as social highlights of the year. People planned for the fairs for months in advance; even the children took on extra chores to earn a little money for fun at the fair.

One old-timer tells a story about a long-time competitor at agricultural fairs who was in the habit of standing by the side of the ring to watch the horses go by. At a strategic point, where the horses turned to face the judge, he would unobtrusively tap a short stick sharply against the boards, causing his opponents' horses to break their stride. This went on for several years, but eventually the chap-with-the-tap and the break-in-the-gait coincided once too often and he was caught in the act.

In the days when horses represented a family's wealth and livelihood, it is not surprising that they were the subjects of many stories and legends. Life itself was affected by the health and abilities of a family's horses – and they were in fact sometimes considered almost members of the family.

One story told by a neighbour concerned his first night on what was to become the family homestead, many years ago. This man had a higher understanding and greater respect for horses than most people, and his own animals were very important to him. His brother, who lived within a short distance of the new homestead, had suggested that he spend the night with him and his family and, as his new home felt very strange and lonely after his first day's work, he decided to take up his brother's invitation. As he strode by the barn, his faithful team whinnied to him. Turning on his heel, he went into the stable to check on their comfort. When he saw them standing uneasily but trustingly in their stalls, he decided that if they could put up with a strange roof over their heads, so could he – and he returned to his own fireside. In all the years that followed, he put the comfort of his fine horses before his own.

Another story came from an elderly woman whose father had been a preacher. At one new charge, her father fell heir to a horse that had belonged to his predecessor. His two daughters had never in their lives harnessed or driven a horse, but the distances to be covered in their new rural surroundings definitely called for a horse and rig. The two girls, with great ingenuity, decided that they could solve their problem with the help of a mail-order catalogue. They carefully studied the pictures in the catalogue and learned the various components of the harness and accoutrements and how they fitted the horse. Even-

tually, they gained enough knowledge to enable them to hitch the harnessed horse to the buggy and drive proudly throughout the countryslde.

A story is told about a man who burst into a rural church, right in the middle of a service, to say that his horses were struggling in quicksand in a nearby mud lake. Without a word, the men in the congregation rushed out of the church to help haul the frantic team to the safety of solid ground. In another instance, a horse fell into an open well close to where a gang was working on the construction of a new road. Immediately, the men in the gang left their work and fell to with their shovels; they dug an approach around the well, so they could walk into it far enough to toss ropes around the immobile beast. With the aid of other horses, they were able to haul him, uninjured, to safety.

At one time an ice plough was used to cut blocks of ice from the river or lake, to be stored in sawdust for summer use. Sometimes the horse pulling the ice plough would slip, struggling, over the edge of the hole where the blocks of ice had been cut and into the icy water. One horseman declared that the safest way to rescue the frightened animal was to throw a slip knot around his neck and pull it tight. Thus, no air could escape from his lungs; he would rise to the top of the water like a balloon and could then be hauled back onto the surface of the ice. This operation would of course have to be accomplished very quickly or the horse would die from lack of air.

In the days of horses, farm work was done in a much more leisurely fashion than it is today. Today's machines need no rest periods, but the horses - and the men walking behind them - did. There was time for a man to pause at the end of a furrow and fill his pipe with a few curls slivered from the plug of tobacco that was usually carried in a back pocket, time to draw in the rich smoke and survey the countryside, perhaps thinking about what to plant in a newly cleared field. Even as he followed his fat sleek team, guiding the plough, a man could find the time to enjoy the fresh air and take pleasure in his land.

Just as horses themselves were considered a sign of a family's substance, the decorations worn by driving horses were symbols of affluence. Ornaments of polished brass were common and they were not only for decorative purposes; they were believed to be lucky amulets. This was especially so of a special ornament, a crescent moon with stars, which was suspended on the horse's forehead to bring good fortune. Ornaments have traditionally been worn by beasts of burden - from camels in Biblical times to elephants in Imperial India - and the horsemen of this country, too, took pride in the adornment of their horses.

Horses were so important to their owners that it took a very special reason for a man to part with one of his beasts. A woman I know treasures a beautiful antique lamp that has been handed down in her family. It seems that, many years ago, her grandfather had traded a valuable horse for the lamp; it was a gift for her grandmother, and the sacrifice he made to give her this gift indicated his great love and respect for her.

An old-time neighbour told a story about some especially fine Clydesdales whose offspring were eagerly sought, as they were considered to come from the best possible stock. The men who owned them used to travel from farm to farm after the harvest, using their teams to press the hay into large bales. By the end of the long season, the teams, as well as the men, were road-worn and weary. One farmer remarked that a team was not up to the usual standards of these noted Clydesdales. The owner was a dramatic character with a dry sense of humour; "Did you see that team of horses at the fair that jumped from a tower into a tank of water?" he drawled in his Irish way. The farmer nodded expectantly. The owner removed the bits from the horses' mouths, drew the halter shanks through the manger rings, and quietly explained, "That's the team!" The farmer replied in amazement, "Gad, Alex, I didn't think I'd ever see the day when I'd stable *that* team!" - as he rushed to fill their mangers with the best hay. Alex grinned to himself and tossed "that team" an extra helping of oats.

There were side advantages to keeping horses. Their manure was of course an excellent fertilizer, especially for the vegetable and flower gardens which were the pride of many farm homes. As well, the manure was often banked against the house in late fall. Covered with snow, it would heat up to provide a real insulation, helping to keep the draughts out of the house. It had to be removed in spring before complete defrosting took place, and the earth under it was then enriched for the planting of a few flowers.

A favourite pastime among farmers and villagers was the game of horseshoes. On summer evenings the metallic ring of a horseshoe hitting the stake echoed through the still air, signalling the skill of the men who often took the game very seriously. The earth around the permanent stake was always well worn, where the horseshoes had fallen as "ringers" or "leaners".

Horses had one great advantage over the "horseless carriages" that eventually took their places: they always knew the way home, no matter how inebriated the driver became on his evening out. They could also find their way home through a blizzard or a dense fog; all the driver had to do was to let his horses have free rein and they would bring him safely home.

One young man learned in a dramatic way to appreciate this attribute of horses. After a visit to his best girl and a drop or two of home brew, he hitched his horse to his "courting buggy" in the dim light of the barnyard and began his homeward journey, full of the warmth of his evening's pleasure. Unknown to him, the girl's two young brothers had secured a cow's skull on a stick at the back of the rig and, as he drove along, he suddenly heard a rattling sound. Glancing back, he was horrified to see hollow eyes staring at him and curved horns bobbing toward him - surely the devil himself. The young man was so startled that all he could do was urge his horse to move a little faster; he was far beyond directing its route. The faster he went, the faster the ghostly creature followed him, until his wise horse led him into his own yard, where he was able to investigate the situation and resolve to take revenge on the prankish youngsters whenever the occasion would present itself.

The courting buggy was, ideally, a black-topped rig, a one-seater, or a more elegant two-seated surrey with a fringe on its canopy that would swing with the motion of the rig. The best were also equipped with storm apron and curtains, but these were only for the well-to-do, or rented for special occasions, in areas where the roads were relatively smooth and well travelled. Rough buggies or road wagons were more common conveyances.

One young suitor was said to have regularly travelled to his intended's house, across a wide river, by "birling" a log - that is, by standing on it and rolling it end over end until he reached the opposite bank. Only once did he get a soaking, according to the storyteller, and that was on the night of a special social event, when he was wearing a new pair of well-waxed boots.

There was a whole mythology surrounding horseshoes in the days when the horse was king. One elderly woman still has a beautiful foot stool in the shape of a horseshoe, a wedding gift to her parents from a blacksmith friend. Seven studs on the stool represent seven horseshoe nails. Were these seven nails simply for the aura of good luck associated with the number seven, and because the arched shape of the horseshoe was thought to denote good fortune? Some blacksmiths maintained that this was nonsense; seven nails would put a horse off balance and do more harm than good. Others insisted that some blacksmiths would use seven nails instead of the usual eight as a corrective measure. It seems clear that some therapeutic shoes were specially forged to hold seven nails; for instance, if a horse "interfered" - that is, scraped one fetlock with the shoe of the other foot - a remedial shoe would be called for.

One old farrier suggested that a too-heavy shoe could sometimes actually cause interfering or striking the other fetlock. This problem could be solved by narrowing and shortening the inside half of the horseshoe, leaving out the quarter nail on that side. Another, younger man offered the information that race horses were sometimes fitted with seven-nailed shoes to facilitate rapid turning on the track. Since this might alter the chances of winning, it could be thought of as a lucky practice.

To prevent "snowballing" - that is, the packing of sticky snow in the cavity of a horse's foot during a long winter drive - one old-time farrier recommended that the soles of the horse's feet be filled with heavy wagon grease to keep the snow from clogging. Otherwise, snowballing was likely to be a great source of discomfort to the horse as well as a nuisance to the driver, who would have to stop and clean out his horse's feet every half mile or so.

Work horses were usually "sharp shod" for winter hauling: sharpened steel "corks" were fitted into their shoes to give them traction on slippery roads or to make it easier for them to haul heavy loads of ice blocks from river or lake.

In later days, horses were used to draw delivery wagons in cities and towns. They usually did most of their work in the early morning hours, travelling from house to house along the streets, hauling their loads of milk, bread, or ice in the brightly painted wagons. Because the sound of their feet on the pavement woke the householders and brought about many complaints, the horses' shoes were usually fitted with rubber "silencers", one and a half inches square and one inch deep, to lessen the noise. Even so, the rhythmic clip-clopping could be heard throughout the neighbourhoods and eventually the horses disappeared from the streets - taking with them the "horse apples" that served as hockey pucks for many a Canadian boy.

However, during World War II, when

cars and gasoline were scarce, horse-drawn delivery wagons were again pressed into service in many towns and villages. In at least one Ontario town today, a horse-drawn wagon is again on the streets, much to the delight of citizens and tourists who enjoy the clip-clopping sounds that were deplored by earlier generations.

Many older people today can recall the first streetcars - horse-drawn cars or buses, with the driver sitting on the outside and the passengers almost as cold on the inside in the bitter winter weather. Hay covered the floors of the streetcars, but in the days when it was considered acceptable to spit on the floor, the vehicles were often quite unsanitary. By the turn of the century most of these horse-drawn cars had been replaced with motorized monstrosities - but it was a long time

before any of them were seen on the streets on Sundays.

In the thirties, when hard times forced many families to use ingenious methods of making-do, there was a wide-spread return to pioneer ways. The old-time horsecar had become all but obsolete long before the Depression, but who could have foreseen the Bennett buggies - cars whose motors were useless because there was no money for gasoline - being pulled by a team of horses which had once again come into their own?

One old man who had farmed through good years and bad - including the "dirty thirties" in Saskatchewan, when the top soil blew from farm to farm and back again - tells a story that reflects conditions and attitudes during the Depression. Not many years ago he unexpectedly received a cheque in payment for a team of horses which he had sold on trust to a fellow rancher during the lean years. The neighbour had recently died and, while clearing out his desk drawer, his wife discovered the bill of sale. Appreciating the fact that the family had been trusted with a team when it was sorely needed almost forty years earlier, she immediately forwarded the amount owing.

In those days when money was short, co-operation between friends and neighbours was the order of the day. One rural family, for instance, had an old buggy in the drive-shed, but no driving horse; a neighbouring family had a "driver" but no buggy. The young people found the obvious solution to the problem and literally put the cart before the horse: the family with the buggy pulled it down the road to the neighbour's farm where it was hitched to the driving horse - and the two families drove off together to pick blueberries to sell in the nearby village.

When the first horseless carriages arrived on the scene, Robert McLaughlin, a manufacturer of horse-drawn vehicles, was strongly opposed to the new-fangled machines. He mounted an advertising campaign to try to convince people that these smelly, noisy vehicles were indeed an invention of the devil. However, it soon became apparent that the automobile was here to stay and, with the attitude "If you can't lick 'em, join 'em," he fell to and began producing the McLaughlin Buick - although he himself preferred to continue driving his horse-drawn carriages.

The automobile brought with it wide-spread changes in lifestyle, but many people, like McLaughlin, accepted the new era with reluctance. The new machines were frightening, especially to older people, and it took a great deal of courage and fortitude to drive the early cars. People complained that they "spooked" the horses - which they certainly did - and they were not as reliable as horses - which they certainly weren't. Tires were a particular problem in the early days; it was taken for granted that they would "blow" every few miles. It was not uncommon for a tire to be changed or refilled several times during a Sunday afternoon drive, while sleek horses shied and raced by - no doubt spurred on by their drivers who looked with scorn on the disabled automobiles.

The early cars were open, not unlike horse-drawn carriages in design, and the roads were dusty, so "dusters" - long, cover-all cloaks - were worn for driving, especially by the ladies. Independent women had long owned and driven spirited horses just as efficiently as men, but when women began to drive motor vehicles, many people were quite horrified. Medical authorities issued dire warnings that the young ladies would ruin the comely shape of their limbs by driving the gas chariots. Working the pedals of a car would be bound to give a lady bulging shins and malformed calves, they said; certainly, it was true that the pedals of the early automobiles were as stiff as tractor clutches.

It was not long before owning an automobile became a matter of prestige, and even the older folk who were often reluctant to drive longed for the glory of ownership. So, although in those days young people did not have much "say" in family decisions, parents who wanted the joy of having a car without the problems of learning how to operate the complicated machinery would allow their sons and daughters to drive them about the countryside. And the older folk, while they were still in awe of the new vehicles, reserved the right to give driving advice and warnings of possible disaster.

One of the greatest problems of early life in the country was the isolation of people whose nearest neighbours might be miles away. The development of improved means of transportation did much to ease this feeling of distance - the building of roads, stronger and more lively horses, and more comfortable carriages all contributed to an easier way of life. The automobile was a great advancement of course, but another development in transportation which cannot be overlooked was the bicycle. It is said that the bicycle craze can be credited with the first real improvements in road conditions. The velocipede - the high, three-wheeled bicycle whose agents boasted "We can beat the swiftest steed/ With our new velocipede" - came into general use before the turn of the century. Soon groups of men and women began to venture out from the towns to explore the countryside, and public demand resulted in smoother roads. But the automobile called for wider, as well as smoother roads, especially in the urban areas, and road-building became a priority.

Still, there were those who wouldn't venture onto the roads, no matter how good they were. Some people who owned cars would sputter around behind the barn or down the back lane - the first cars were built very high off the ground, to avoid ruts, rocks, and roosters! - but that is as far as they would go. There are stories about new owners who used their automobiles to drive the hundred yards or so between house and backhouse. Perhaps

some of them looked upon this as driving practice, but others were just lazy.

Most of those who did drive cars in the early days were fair-weather drivers only. The back roads were blocked with snow from November till mid-April, and then were muddy for at least another month. But a horse, pulling a buggy or sleigh, could still make its way over terrain that was impossible for an automobile. It is little wonder that many people saw motor vehicles as senseless contraptions - there was so much evidence that horse-drawn carriages were superior.

One old neighbour bought a car that was years old but in perfect condition. The previous owners, two bachelors, had used it only on summer Sundays - and they hadn't ever gone anywhere in it. They would sit in it and spin the wheels each Sunday, jack it up on blocks in the fall, replace the wheels each spring, and again go for a stationary ride each Sunday during the summer. They never did work up enough courage to experiment with the gear shift and back it out of the driving shed.

This kind of story was not uncommon. Another pair of brothers bought a car and, when it was delivered, they instructed the dealer to leave it in the drive shed beside the horse-drawn carriages. According to a neighbour they would climb into the car twice a week and spin the wheels for half an hour or so. But when they really wanted to go somewhere, the horse and carriage always won out.

This nervousness about driving was not without reason. Many were the stories about new drivers who shifted into the wrong gear with disastrous results. One new car owner was so excited with his purchase that when he stepped on the gas he couldn't control his foot and the car shot right through the barn door into a straw stack. After that he was too frightened to take any risks with it, and eventually a neighbour bought it and enjoyed it for many years.

Another old man was a great procrastinator when it came to driving his new car. Soon after he got it he decided it was time to put it up on blocks for the winter. In the spring he bought a licence for it and had his sons make sure it was roadworthy. But he always found some excuse not to take it out, although he would walk around it, checking it and kicking the tires every day. One day he returned to the house, sucking on his pipe, and announced triumphantly that the old red hen had nested in the back seat, so he would have to wait until the chicks were hatched before moving the "autymobile".

Coughs and Colds and the Spectre of Death

Care to our coffin adds a nail, no doubt,
And every grin so merry draws one out.

- Dr. Walcott, 1739-1819

In the earlier days in Canada, death seemed much closer than it does to most people today. The advance of medicine has virtually spelled the end of many diseases that were commonplace in our grandparents' and great grandparents' time - although there does not seem to have been much progress in the search for a cure for the common cough and cold. People used to have many ways of dealing with infections and diseases; doctors were not always available, and even if there was a physician who could be called, his wisdom was often considered not much greater than that of an old grandmother who had nursed two or three generations through all kinds of illnesses.

Smallpox, almost unknown today, was a dangerous and often fatal disease not too many years ago. Periodic smallpox epidemics swept farm to village to town; a common adage said, "From smallpox and love, but few remain free." To ward off smallpox germs, powdered sulphur was burned in a room or sulphur candles were lit and left burning until their fumes had supposedly destroyed all the germs that were lurking about in the air. As the fumes of burning sulphur were poisonous to man and beast, both people and pets were barred from the room while this treatment was being administered. The powdered sulphur was sometimes just thrown on the top of the hot wood stove, but some homes had special jars for burning it. One family I know still has a "smallpox jar" - a hand-painted crockery jar in which earlier members of the family had habitually burned sulphur in an effort to curb the disease.

A cough and a sniffle could signal the onset of a common cold, but they might also be the first symptoms of something far more serious, so they were usually looked upon with some concern. But there were always a few people whose sudden symptoms were brought on by a devastating thirst, and a drop or two of "the medicine" was thought to be the only immediate, if temporary, cure. This was in the days when most of polite society gave lip service to the belief that alcohol was to be used only for medicinal purposes - so a thirsty soul had to plead sickness in order to justify a tot of brandy. However, small hotels could usually be found only a mile or two apart on the early roads - a fact which must have broken the resolve of many a would-be teetotaller. Bad roads, which were difficult to travel in winter blizzards, muddy spring thaws, and summer storms, made the hotels a necessary evil or a godsend, depending upon one's point of view.

A hot toddy was no doubt helpful to someone suffering from the cold but, taken in excess, it could and often did have dangerous consequences, especially to someone who had to walk any distance in bad weather. One family tells a story about an old gentleman who, after partaking a little too freely of the medicine, took a shortcut home in the darkness across the ice. But there had recently been a slight thaw and the ice was not as strong as it might have been. The inevitable happened - the old man suddenly found himself in the water. Fortunately, one arm rested on

a solid edge of ice so he did not sink completely. After a number of hours in the icy water he was hauled out by an early-rising neighbour who heard his cries, bundled up in carriage blankets, and rushed to a doctor. The limbs that had been under water suffered little damage, but the arm that had been exposed to the frosty air had to be amputated.

The fear of drowning was ever present, as swollen streams and rivers often had to be crossed and the flimsy bridges were repeatedly washed out by storms. Open wells were another common hazard. One family tells of the frightening time a toddler fell into a thirty-foot well. The child's mother became so hysterical that she was immobilized, but the grandmother climbed down and rescued the apparently lifeless child. In desperation she held the child upside down and secured her, by her feet, to the clothesline. This ingenious treatment allowed the water to drain from the child's lungs and she survived the ordeal; the story, not surprisingly, has been handed down in the family for generations.

Drowning victims were sometimes lain stomach down over a barrel and rolled back and forth until the water drained from the lungs. According to stories that have been told, these unscientific methods of artificial respiration were often as effective as the more modern methods in general use today.

Accidents of all kinds had to be dealt with quickly with whatever materials were at hand. A burn could be treated with the beaten white of an egg, mixed with a tablespoon of lard and applied to the burned flesh. If an insect flew into a child's ear, the recommended treatment was to pour a little melted butter into the ear and follow it with a rinse of luke-warm water to flush the pest out. A painful insect bite was often treated with the juice of a fresh lemon, if one was available. In an emergency, the flow of blood could be checked by flour: when a farm harrow passed over the driver of a runaway team of horses, the jagged cuts were treated with flour and they healed beautifully. Buckwheat flour was best for this purpose, because of its rutin content - although most people probably did not know why it was best, only that it did the trick more effectively than other kinds of flour.

Some children were subject to convulsions, a terrifying experience for the parents. To bring him out of his frightening fit, the child was plunged into warm water. In the winter there was usually a large cauldron of water warming on the back of the stove, but in summer the barrel of rain water at the corner of the house was warm enough to be used as a quick plunge bath to bring down the fever and relieve the child of the convulsion.

Another hazard of country life was the ever-present poison ivy, which frequently grew among blueberries; blueberry-picking expeditions were often followed by the agony of fiercely itching skin caused by the juices of the innocuous-looking plant. This could sometimes be prevented by lathering the skin well with strong soap before starting out, but if the inevitable happened, relief could be found in the application of plantain root or salt dissolved in buttermilk.

In the early days, swamps were sources of infection and fever, as they provided an ideal breeding ground for disease-carrying mosquitoes and insects. Swamp fever was a fearful malady, sometimes fatal, and a common and frequently effective treatment for it was the bark of a choke-cherry tree, infused in whiskey and taken internally by the delirious sufferer.

A few years ago a gang of road workers unearthed two skeletons in the course of their digging. An investigation was launched: were the two perhaps native Indians, or was there any indication that a double murder had been committed? Understandably, there was much talk about the mystery, and speculation was rife. Then an elderly lady told a friend that she didn't want to talk to the authorities about it, but she knew the origin of the skeletons. They had been found on her family's homestead where, over a century ago, road workers had suddenly come down with "the fever" while clearing a swamp to make way for a new road. Two of the workers had died and, in order to cut down the chances of an epidemic, permission had been granted to have the victims buried immediately on the land where they had died. The story had of course been passed down in the woman's family, and so the mystery was solved.

Another of the most dreaded diseases in the earlier days was hydrophobia, or rabies, caused by the bite of a mad dog or other animal. Today this disease, when it occurs, is treated with a series of painful shots, but home nurses used to have a number of ways of caring for patients who had become the unfortunate victims of this horrendous infection. Vapour baths, with strong solutions of ammonia or unfusions of the elecampane or horseheal plant, were administered. Elecampane, a coarse herb of the aster family, has been used medicinally since the time of Hippocrates; as its alternate name suggests, the roots have long been considered effective medicine for horses. A potion of elecampane, taken internally, was also used for the treatment of rabies: the recipe called for one and a half ounces of the root of the plant, either green or dried, bruised and placed in a jar with a pint of fresh milk. This was boiled down to half volume, strained, and drunk by the patient, who then had to fast for at least six hours. This treatment was repeated for three mornings and, if followed exactly, was said to be a sure cure.

An elderly friend told me a story about a young child who had been badly bitten by a dog. After weeks of treatment, the wound still refused to heal and the child's family was in despair. Finally, a ninety-four year old woman announced that there was one more remedy to be tried. She stripped some bark from an elm tree - presumably slippery elm, which was considered to have medicinal properties - and scraped a jelly-like substance from the wood underneath. Shortly after this was applied to the wound, the healing process began and continued apace.

But the common cold and the complications that sometimes resulted from it seemed to cause the most concern among the people of earlier days - no one was untouched by the seasonal cold, and the risks were often great when any of the dreaded complications set in. Some of the remedies used in days gone by seem to make at least as much sense as many of those in use today. From rose-petal or rose-hip tea to a spoonful of skunk oil, the recommended remedies ranged from the sublime to the ridiculous. When a child came down with an attack of croup, for example, and medical advice was just not available, skunk oil was often administered. The taste and smell of this revolting substance was almost certain to cause vomiting, and thus the smothering phlegm would be eliminated - so perhaps the remedy was not as ridiculous as it seems.

One elderly woman claims that she was able to save many a croupy child with "pee and goose grease". A mixture of equal quantities of goose oil and urine, in a dose ranging from a teaspoon to a tablespoon depending on the age of the child and repeated every fifteen minutes if necessary, was guaranteed to produce the same results as skunk oil.

Patients with coughs and colds were advised to "feed a cold and starve a fever," to inhale hot water and turpentine for influenza, to soak their feet in a tub of hot water with red pepper and mustard, and to chew spruce gum or sip a pinch of dried ginger in a cup of very hot water to ease the discomfort of a sore throat. To relieve a cough, one prescription called for two ounces of balm of Gilead buds in two quarts of soft water, simmered down to a volume of one pint, and administered by the tablespoon as required. For adults, another mixture was often given in a wine glass: two ounces of balm of Gilead buds and four ounces of sugar infused in a quart of rum. This was kept on hand in many homes during the cold season; it was said to be more effective after it had "set" for a few days.

A blend of lemon and honey was one of the more pleasant-tasting cough remedies; others were needles of a pine tree, simmered with sugar in water, and licorice tea, which was said to be more effective if drunk when it was cold. Many herbs were also used with considerable success for coughs and colds. Thyme, summer savoury, or leaves of the coltsfoot plant were infused as soothing teas. Even nettle foliage was said to relieve bronchial congestion when steeped in hot water.

Many people believed that an effective remedy for a cough and scratchy throat was a wool sock, wrapped around the neck and secured with a safety pin. The sock was usually foul smelling, either from some home liniment mixture or because it had been taken directly from contact with a sweaty foot - the smellier the sock, the more effective the treatment, it appears.

To stop a sneezing fit, the patient was advised to slowly sip three or four table-spoons of hot milk between sneezes. Fever blisters were relieved by the application of fresh turnip scrapings, every four hours both day and night.

The older people often stated that the more bitter the medicine, the more effec-tive it would be. But in spite of this belief, some of the recommended remedies were sweet and pleasant to taste. Elderberry syrup and currant jelly were both prescribed for coughs; another turn-of-the-century remedy for colds was a very sweet mixture indeed. This recipe called for two cups of molasses with a small spoonful of dried ginger and a half cup of butter. This was simmered for about half an hour and then two tablespoons of vinegar or the juice of two warm lemons would be added; the mixture was covered and left on the back of the stove and sipped as needed, warm or cold. The sweet, spicy syrup was undoubtedly a very soothing treatment for a raw throat.

Another sweet remedy was called Indian cough syrup; it was made from the roots of the elecampane plant and Indian turnip, or jack-in-the-pulpit. Half an ounce of each of these was bruised and mixed with two cups of honey, steeped thoroughly and strained. Taken in small doses as often as required, this concoction was advocated as an effective throat-ease.

Another old-time treatment brought immediate relief from a paroxysm of coughing. This consisted of one or two tablespoons of glycerine, mixed with hot, rich cream or pure whiskey, according to the age, taste, and outlook of the patient as well as the availability of either ingredient.

A lemon gargle was recommended for diphtheria patients, and flaxseed lemonade was a popular treatment for colds. The flaxseed was boiled down in water until it became a thick syrup; it was strained through a cloth and mixed with a quarter pound of loaf sugar and a little lemon juice. A note on the recipe said it was "very serviceable" for relieving colds. However, lemons were both scarce and expensive, so these remedies could be enjoyed only by fairly affluent people.

When kidneys were affected by a severe cold, yarrow infused as a tea was the treatment of choice; although it was bitter tasting, it was considered highly effective. Mullein leaves, saturated in hot vinegar, were sometimes placed in warm flannel and applied to painful swollen glands; dried mullein leaves were often smoked in a pipe to ease throat irritation, according to one old timer. Grated ginger root and horehound, simmered with a bit of molasses, made a syrup that was soothing to sufferers of whooping cough, and catnip prepared in the same way was taken to ease the pain of an inflamed throat. Another treatment for a sore throat was a piece of salt pork heated in vinegar.

An old French cure for the 'flu called for one teaspoon of powdered ginger, the juice of a lemon, and two teaspoons of honey, dissolved in a cup of hot water. The patient was advised to "go to bed and sweat it out."

Some of the more distasteful preparations for treating a bad cough included a mixture of turpentine and warm goose or skunk oil, rubbed on the chest to ease congestion, and a few drops of kerosene soaked into a spoonful of brown sugar and swallowed to silence a persistent cough. This last could be a very powerful dose if not carefully administered, as one young lad discovered. He was visiting a cousin, and while the two boys were alone in the house, he developed a sore throat and a wracking cough. The lads both remem-

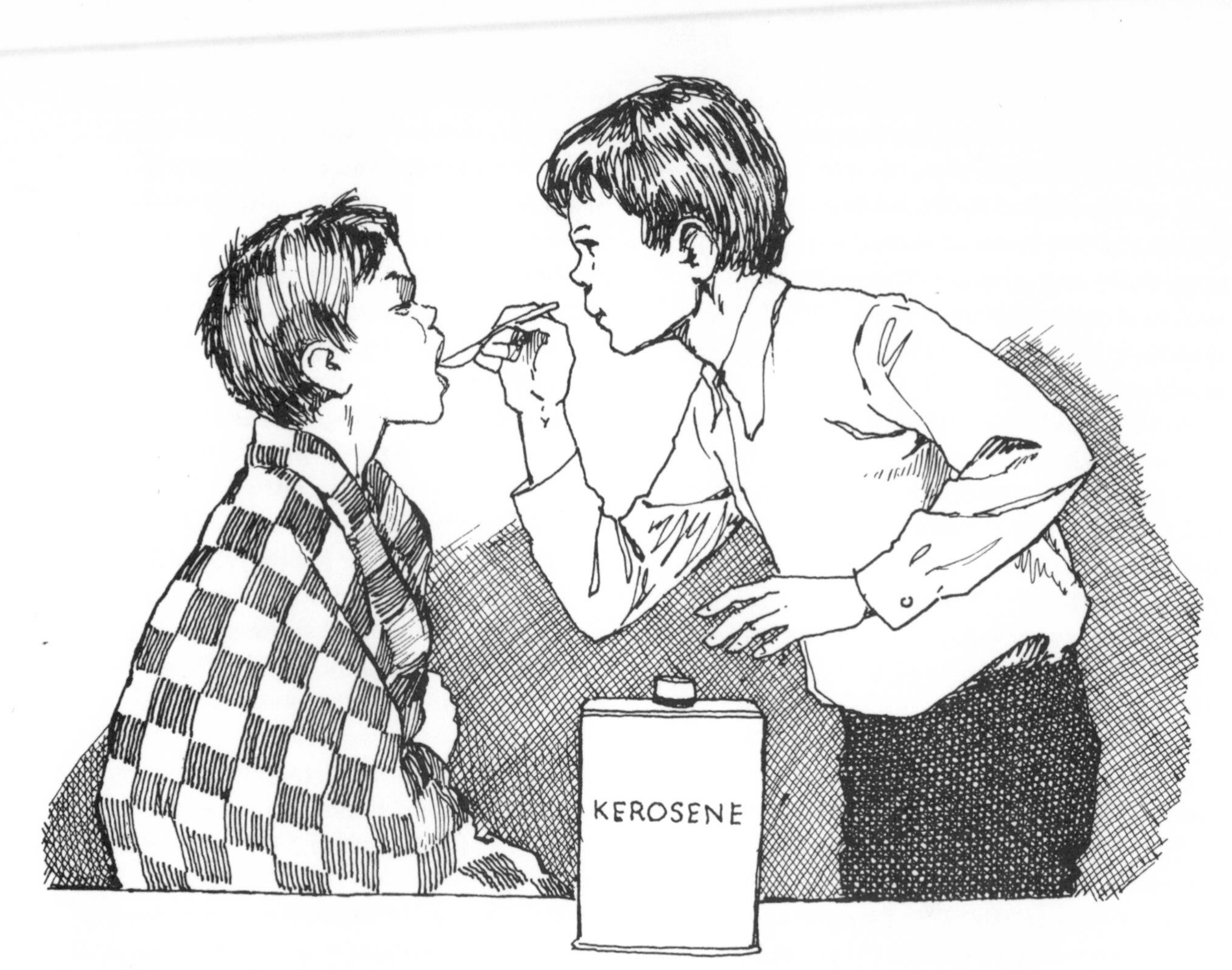

bered hearing that kerosene was sometimes and somehow used as a remedy for such symptoms, so they decided it was worth trying. They reasoned that if a small dose was beneficial, a double dose would be twice as effective, and as they were both anxious that the visitor be in good shape before the adults returned, they poured out a full teaspoon of kerosene and, closing his eyes, the sick boy gulped it down. "It darn near killed me!" he later vowed, recalling the fiery throat and dizziness which followed.

It seems more than likely that a number

of deaths were actually caused by some of the substances used as the drugs of earlier days. It was often a case of "kill or cure" and most people did not realize the potency of such medicines - not just household items like kerosene, but also real medicines like quinine, opium, belladonna, foxglove, or the May apple, all of which were quite widely used.

But many of the remedies used, if they did no real good, certainly did no harm, and both patient and home nurse benefitted from the belief that something was being done. Chicken jelly, for instance, was often prescribed for a sick person. A chicken was boiled for several hours in a little water and the liquid was then strained through a jelly bag. Salt was added and the liquid was chilled until it jelled. It was a soft and nourishing dish for a sick person, and it slid down a sore throat painlessly.

Preventive medicine in earlier days included such tonics as Irish moss. This product was available in non-Maritime provinces from the apothecary and was used to make a type of blanc mange. It was cooked in milk in a double boiler with a drop or two of flavouring added as it cooled, then set in a mould or individual dishes and decorated with a sprinkling of nutmeg. This concoction was taken regularly in some homes and was believed to ward off all manner of illness. Onions and garlic were also used freely in the daily diet to ensure health. In seasons when childhood diseases had reached epidemic proportions, conscientious mothers protected children with cubes of camphor, sewn into pieces of flannelette around their necks or pinned to their undershirts.

Chronically ill patients were, if possible, given a room with a southern exposure, in the belief that the greater amount of sunlight in such a room would be beneficial. However, some families had a superstitious belief that pestilence came from the south, so their houses were built with no windows on the south side. I know of one old farmhouse that was at least a century old before a window was cut in its southern wall.

It has always been said that when a patient becomes cranky and demanding, he is on the way to recovery. A certain cure for naughty speech in restless children was the old wash-out-the-mouth-with-soap routine. The lye soap that was in common use no doubt discouraged the child from repeating his unacceptable behaviour, but it was also a safeguard against germs for weeks to come.

Aching and tired feet were often a problem in the days when people walked a

lot more than most do now, and old people particularly often complained that they had "bad feet" or that their feet were "done" - they even sometimes described themselves as "footless". Tired feet were sometimes treated with the application of eel fat, which was supposed to have a soothing effect. Another remedy which was thought to reduce the discomfort of tired and aching feet was a mixture of one table-spoon of salt, a "fig" of tobacco, and a pint of urine. These ingredients were simmered together and applied with a sponge at bedtime.

Death was never too far from the minds of our grandparents and great grand-parents and, as they grew older, it became more and more a matter to be faced squarely. One dear old lady, well into her eighties, used to curl her hair faithfully every night. She knew that she might "go at any time" and she remembered that a friend of hers had passed away suddenly, without her hair properly coiffed. She thought that her friend had looked "just terrible" in her coffin, and she had resolved that the same thing would not happen to her.

It was often said that when one person died, an infant would soon be born into the family circle. In the days when large fami-lies were the rule rather than the excep-tion, there was a good deal of truth in this belief.

Work was considered the best antidote for loneliness, worry, and sorrow. A mother who lost a child almost always had other children who were dependent on her and so she kept going, with little time out for grieving. A good cry was allowed, but women were advised never to weep with their corsets on - which made sound medical sense. And men, of course, were expected never to give into their sorrow, at least not in public.

Many people believed that tears were nature's strongest germ killers; one teaspoon of tears was said to give antisep-tic power to as much as a hundred gallons of water. A story is told in my family about an old lady who had become almost blind before the death of her husband. Shortly after his death, she regained her eyesight to such an extent that she could thread a needle without the aid of her spectacles. The old people said simply that she had "gotten her second sight". The family doctor claimed that she had shed so many tears over the death of her husband that their healing power had restored her sight.

Kettles and Kindling

And homeless, near a thousand homes I stood
And near a thousand tables pined and wanted food.

In most Canadian homes in earlier days, the kitchen was a veritable hive of activity. The kitchen was really the room where a family lived - it was large and, in the cold winter months, the warmest room in the house. It had a fireplace or a black monster of a cookstove, where a pot of delicious smelling soup or stew simmered almost constantly. It had a large table, often made of white pine wood, around which the family gathered to eat, chat, and work. In the early evening, the children of the family would do their homework at the kitchen table, while mother and grandmother mended clothes or knitted, and father and grandfather busied themselves repairing a broken harness or reading a newspaper. Most kitchens had a couch in a corner where a sick member of the family could rest within the family circle, and the baby's cradle, too, was likely to be in the kitchen, where the mother could keep a watchful eye on the sleeping child.

A fixture on most kitchen tables was the molasses jug. Molasses was the cheapest and most common sweetener, and the old saying "as slow as molasses in January" brings back recollections of the days when, in the most bitter winter weather, even the big kitchen stove could not keep the room warm enough for the molasses to "run". Molasses really came into its own in the spring when a crock of the thick syrup, mixed with powdered sulphur and a little cream of tartar, took its seasonal place on the back lid of the big kitchen stove. The unappetizing yellowish grey mixture was considered a tonic, blood thinner, and purifier that would act as an internal cleanser and energizer after the long months of winter. The prescription no doubt varied from one home to another, but the general rule was that a "good spoonful" would be taken by every member of the family for nine days; they would skip three days and then repeat the nine-day siege.

There was a common belief that it was dangerous to get your feet wet during the sulphur-and-molasses treatment, but an elderly friend tells a story about one old man who used to down the tonic religiously each spring and then go sloshing through the mud and water in defiance of such a silly belief. Apparently he never suffered any after-effects from this risky practice.

Another tonic that was traditional in many homes was a dose of castor oil. If a child looked the least bit "peakish", some adult in the family was sure to say, "What that youngster needs is a good dose of castor oil!" The nasty-tasting liquid was sometimes combined with the yolk of a fresh egg and a little water, sugar, and grated nutmeg to make it more palatable. Taken alone, it was an experience to remember; one woman who, as a child, had always been given a slice of orange as a chaser after her dose vowed that she had not been able to look an orange in the face ever since.

Molasses, of course, was much more than the major ingredient in a spring tonic. It was said to be good for removing the sting from a burn and a teacup of molasses, poured into a pail of whitewash, was believed to help the whitewash penetrate into wood or plaster. Molasses was often eaten alone as a dessert and was used as a sweetener in many receipts, including these two.

Simple Molasses Candy

one cup molasses
one cup sugar
one tablespoon vinegar
butter the size of an egg

Boil but do not stir until the mixture will harden in cold water. Stir in a teaspoon of soda. Pour onto a buttered surface to cool. Pull into twisted strands until it becomes lighter in colour.

Dr. Chase's Rough and Ready Cakes

one pound butter or lard
one quart molasses
one ounce soda
one-half pint milk or water
one tablespoon ground ginger
oil of lemon
"sufficient" flour

Mix ginger in flour and rub in the butter or lard. Dissolve soda in milk or water, put in molasses, and use the flour in which the ginger and butter are rubbed up, and sufficient more to make the dough of a proper consistency to roll out. Cut the cakes out with a long and narrow cutter and wet the top with a little molasses and water to remove the flour from the cake. Turn the top down into well-ground white sugar and place in the oven sufficiently hot for bread, but keep the cakes in only enough to bake, not to dry up. This is a great favourite where they know what is good and have the means to make it; yet it is not expensive.

Another sweet liquid that was highly prized was maple syrup. Where maple trees grew in abundance they were tapped in the late winter, and for a few weeks a large pot of sap would be simmering on the old kitchen stove. One woman tells of her grandfather, after his springtime bath, dropping his winter "combinations" into what he thought was the kettle of rainwater for preboiling the clothes before laundering. He hadn't looked or smelled carefully enough, and it is not hard to imagine what the underwear did for the maple syrup - or what the maple syrup did for the underwear.

In earlier days the weekly baking was a big event in a family's life, involving several members of the family and taking many hours. Cakes, puddings, and cookies were prepared in quantity; nuts had to be shelled, dried fruits washed and picked over, spices ground, and all had to be chopped and stirred together thoroughly. The old kitchen was full of delicious smells on baking day, and even the smallest children stood by to help lick out the mixing bowls. Special receipts were handed down from one generation to another and many housewives took pride in making the occasional elaborate offering. One favourite receipt was said to have come from the royal kitchen of Queen Victoria.

Royal Plum Pudding

two pounds currants
two pounds large Valencia raisins, seeded
two pounds suet
two pounds dark brown sugar
two pounds bread crumbs
two pounds apples, finely chopped
two pounds lemons, rind and juice
whole nutmegs, grated
one-half pound mixed peel, lemon, citron, and orange
one and one-half pounds flour
one teaspoon salt
eight eggs
one-half pint each of brandy, port, sherry, and new milk

Boil for six hours and again for two hours before serving.

Needless to say, a receipt such as this was only made for Christmas, or other very special occasions, and only in the more well-to-do homes. In most homes there were many mouths to feed and the food was usually quite plain. The following receipts are examples of typical daily fare.

Great Aunt Sally's Flannel Cakes

two pints flour
enough milk to make a light batter
pinch of salt
lump of melted butter
five or six eggs, beaten

Stir ingredients together and bake on a griddle over a fireplace or in a heavy frying pan over a wood stove. Serve with honey or molasses.

Backwoods Preserves

Gently boil a pint of molasses for about 15 minutes. Quickly stir in three good-sized eggs, well beaten. Simmer a few minutes longer, stirring constantly. Season with grated nutmeg.

Herbs and spices were used a good deal to heighten flavour or perhaps, in some cases, to hide it. Herbs were grown locally, but spices had to be imported, so were highly treasured and carefully used. They were usually stored in tightly sealed containers in a dark place so they would retain their flavour and power. Spices such as nutmeg, ginger, and cinnamon were ground or grated just before use, so they would be as fresh as possible.

The return of the wild geese in the spring often meant a welcome change in diet for farm families of earlier days. The old expression "the goose hangs high" suggested a measure of prosperity; if a goose was hung to be smoked in the chimney, the family had enough food and did not need the goose for immediate consumption. A wild goose was said to "smell to high heaven" while it was being cooked; the tart smell of the high bush cranberries which were usually cooked as an accompaniment for game probably balanced out the odour of the goose. Some families kept domestic geese as well; these had to be kept out of the grain fields, so the lead gander was often fitted with a "poke" - three slats nailed together in a triangle and slipped around his neck - as a restraining measure.

The dehydrated convenience foods that are so common today had their counterparts in much earlier times. In the days when travelling was slow and exhausting, people often took food with them on a journey. Ingenious housewives would make a good thick vegetable soup and simmer it down until most of the liquid was gone. It could then be carried easily, and when the traveller got hungry he could add water from a stream or well to make himself a quick lunch, along with some form of hardtack, with johnny cake (journey cake) for dessert. Old-time housewives also placed sliced fruits on racks to dry in the summer sun; these could be enjoyed all winter when fresh fruits were not available.

In days gone by, people welcomed strangers into their homes much more readily than most do now. Travel was difficult and slow, and people going from one place to another needed to rest and eat on the way; a stranger in the house meant an interesting break in routine, certainly news, and possibly even some entertainment for the family. Visitors were received in the kitchen, too, and invited to share the family board. Some housewives kept a kettle of what they called "charitable soup" simmering on the stove, with vegetables and other morsels being added almost every day. In one home there was a frequent visitor, an old man who just happened to arrive before mealtime on most of his calls. He always enjoyed the soup that was served to him. As the family was large, the food was put out on the table on broad platters in heaping bowls. During one of his visits the old man sat down at the table and reached for the gravy boat. Setting it on his plate, he proceeded to spoon up the contents with enthusiasm, while the amused members of the family politely ignored his faux pas. When he had finished the last drop, he set the empty bowl aside and exclaimed, with great appreciation, "That was good soup, ma'am".

Hungry strangers were seldom turned away from the door, but sometimes they were expected to answer certain questions before food was offered to them. On one occasion, a would-be guest was given the usual interrogation: "Would you be willing to work if you could get it?" "Oh, yes indeed, ma'am." "And would you be willing to chop an armful of wood before you leave?" "Yes, ma'am, I'd be glad to." "And would you be taking a little drink?" "Oh, yes, ma'am, I wouldn't mind that at all!" But, in this household at least, the last question was a trap, and the poor man was sent away with nothing more than a drink of cold water from the wooden pump and a pious sermon on the evils of laziness and drink.

Another story concerns a young person who appeared one day at a farmhouse door, dusty and weary from the road. This was during the Depression years when it was common for men to walk from one town to another or "ride the rails" to look for the work that was almost impossible to find. These travellers were always taken in, no questions asked, and fed at the family table. This visitor went to the sink to freshen up before the meal and, as the

peaked cap came off, waist-length blonde hair came tumbling out. The story came out too: the young woman had received word that her father was gravely ill, many miles away; as she had no money for bus or train fare, she was hiking along the railway track to her destination. The peaked cap and sturdy work shirt and pants added to her comfort and concealed her sex, so she could make this daring trip in relative safety.

In some ways, sex roles were not as clearly defined in earlier days as we might think. The women on farms were often called upon to help with the chores and even the harvesting, and the boys and men were usually willing to do such "women's work" as rocking the baby or churning the butter. One enterprising young man figured out a way of doing these two jobs at once; he set a jar of cream at the foot of the cradle and, while the baby was lulled to sleep, the cream was churned into butter.

Butter churning was a tiresome task that had to be done every week or so. If the cream were too cold, it took a very long time for the butter globules to form in the churn. In an old family diary there is an account of a particular day when "the butter must have been bewitched" because it refused to "come". Many people believed that if a red-hot poker were dipped into the cream it would drive the evil spirit away and allow the butter to form. The truth is, of course, that the poker would warm the cream, and that made all the difference.

Before the turn of the last century, an Ontario housewife and dairywoman sold her prize-winning butter on the New York market for a dollar a pound, at a time when the Ontario price was about twenty-five cents. Because she was determined that more women should take part in the business of agriculture, she wrote a book entitled *Dairying for Profit*, dedicating it to "my sisters in toil". In it she explained the intricacies of choosing a cow, feeding it, churning the butter, and keeping accounts; her work did much to raise the prestige of farm women.

Women had little choice but to be enterprising in the days when household necessities were not easily affordable at the general store. Pedlars used to call at farm homes, bringing an array of treasures, but their calls were infrequent and unpredictable. Such commonplace items as candle-wicking often had to be made in the farm kitchen, and then the wicks were carefully dipped, over and over again, or they were placed in long, thin moulds which were then filled with beeswax or tallow. The wicking was made from twisted linen or cord, soaked in a solution of borax, coarse salt, and water. When the material was saturated the strands were separated from each other and hung to dry for several days. Eventually kerosene lamps replaced candles in most homes, but candles were usually stored away for emergencies, just as in later years the coal-oil lamps were kept on hand in case of a power failure.

During the Depression years, salesmen pestered people as poor as themselves, knocking on kitchen doors in the hope of making a sale and earning a bit of money. But money was scarce everywhere, and most families struggled to make do with what they had, restoring furniture and remaking clothing. The salesmen, ragmen, and pedlars were often a nuisance and an embarrassment, as the housewives would hate to turn them down; one woman, when asked if she had had the ragman call, replied, "No, and I'm glad of it because we've nothing but rags and we can't part with them."

Farm wives helped each other by exchanging household hints and sharing their useful discoveries with their friends. One would suggest adding salt to the starch to keep an iron from sticking; another woman would tell her friend to iron ribbons by smoothing them back and forth around a hot stovepipe or over the edge of a heated iron. Doilies should be washed in a jar of hot, sudsy water, shaken vigorously, and then wrapped around a bottle to dry, so the delicate lace would not be damaged; they should then be stored on a covered cardboard tube to prevent creasing. Salt should be sprinkled on the bottom of the oven and bran on the bottom of the cake tin, to keep the cake from burning.

In a corner of the kitchen, or perhaps in the woodshed behind the kitchen, there was often a furniture-restoring project in progress. Furniture was painted and repainted until, eventually, someone decided it should be stripped back to the

bare wood. A mixture that was guaranteed to take off anything consisted of a thin, soupy flour-and-water paste to which lye was added very carefully to the strength required. When the paste was thin enough, it was put into an agate or iron utensil and allowed to settle before being spread on the furniture to be stripped.

When children behaved badly, many mothers and fathers thought that the best cure was a "trip to the woodshed". Old-timers from many different areas of the country have vowed that the order, "To the woodshed with you!" put more youngsters on the straight and narrow path than any other means of punishment. To add insult to injury, the young lad - girls seem to have received more genteel treatment in most homes - was often sent to cut his own switch, to be applied with parental firmness to the seat of the pants. Perhaps it was little wonder that one young boy, on hearing his mother tell a pedlar that she wanted to buy a switch, headed for parts unknown. How was he to know that she meant a switch of hair to add to her coiffure?

A pinch of dry mustard on the tongue of a rude child was another common remedy but, in all fairness to mothers, they were even quicker, when a child bit his tongue, to give him a pinch of sugar to ease the pain, check the bleeding, and promote healing - or simply as a soothing treat. Brown sugar was also sprinkled on the back of a wood stove lid during an epidemic. The scorching sugar was believed to have a germicidal effect on the air of the house and this has since been given scientific approval.

Horseradish, as well as being used as a condiment, was thought to be the most effective treatment for clearing stuffed sinuses. One young boy, watching his grandmother preparing the parsnip-like root for pickling, pestered her for a taste of it. Finally she gave in, cautioning him about its power. Heedlessly, he took a good spoonful and immediately appreciated the wisdom of his grandmother's warning. Three bounding circles of the farm kitchen were required before he could rid himself of the fire in his mouth. The first circle around the big table with smarting eyes, nose, and throat, found him unable to halt; on the second round he grabbed the dipper hanging on the water pail; and on the third circle he was able to snatch a scoop of throat-easing well water from the pail.

The Party Line

Who'll bring a bone will take one,
Great Grandma used to say . . .
Who'll bring a bone of gossip
Will carry one away.

- Author unknown

The advent of the telephone probably had a greater impact on the lives of families on isolated farms than any other development. Loneliness was eased when a housewife could, from her own kitchen, talk to a neighbour several miles away who was also in her own kitchen. The arrival of the telephone also brought with it a measure of safety: if someone was sick or injured, a doctor could be called; if a fire broke out, help could be quickly summoned. The telephone became a bearer of good news and bad, lively chatter and idle gossip. But most of all it was *there* in an emergency, lending a feeling of security and support to people who had been accustomed to living in a constant state of isolation. It was a source of wonder and delight - and also, for some people, a source of fear and apprehension.

There are many stories about the strange reactions of people who had "just got the telephone in". One man was "death against" the new-fangled contraption and, when a telephone was installed in his home, he refused to have anything to do with it. Usually some other member of the family was on hand to answer it, but one evening they all went out to visit neighbours and he was left at home alone. His family decided to call home, just for fun. In the early days, a caller simply cranked out the number of rings assigned to the party being called. The family, knowing how their father hated the telephone, rang the number again and again. Finally they heard the click of the telephone receiver being picked up; a gruff voice boomed out, "There's nobody home!" and the receiver was replaced with a bang.

Another man didn't like to answer the phone or even call a neighbour as long as someone else was willing to perform the chore. One day, however, the family set off for a funeral, dressed in their Sunday best. As they drove down the long farm lane they saw a cow which had broken through a fence and was foraging in the corn field – every herd seemed to have one "breachy" member. If she was not soon removed, the rest of the herd would follow her, mooing all the way. Rather than risk getting their good clothes dirty, the family stopped at the first farmhouse down the road and called home to tell their father about the problem. After much ringing, the telephone was answered in an overly polite, scarcely recognizable voice that their father had adopted as the special way of speaking on this strange new instrument that "talked at you" from the wall.

A story is told about a woman who was also very uncomfortable with the telephone. When some friends were visiting her one evening, they heard the telephone ringing with her special ring. She completely ignored it, and her friends said, "That's your ring," probably looking forward to hearing some news or gossip. "Oh, you answer it!" she entreated. "No, no," they insisted, "It's your ring; somebody wants to talk to you." In a fluster, the woman took off her apron, smoothed her hair, and went to answer the telephone.

Although there were a few people like these who found the telephone a rather frightening and intimidating invention, most people took great delight in the entertainment and interest that the ringing box brought into their lives. In the early days, of course, all lines were party lines, so it was possible to listen to other people's conversations.

There were three types of people on the party line: the "hello-and goodbye-thank-goodness-that's-over" type, the "visiting" type, and the "listener" who perhaps seldom used the telephone but enjoyed a second-hand conversation. To many it was a delight to sit in the rocking chair and listen to another family member chatting on the "contraption". If the voice on the other end of the line carried well – as it often did, because many people seemed to think it was necessary to shout over the telephone - both sides of the conversation would be audible in a quiet room.

Then, of course, there was the chronic, addicted listener who, as people used to say, "never missed a ring". One old gentleman used to lift the receiver every time he passed the telephone, just in case he might have missed somebody calling out - in which case the ring was not heard on the home line. "Listening in" was a great source of entertainment, especially for shut-ins who sometimes chimed in on a conversation, perhaps to tell the caller that so-and-so has gone out of town, so there's no use trying to reach him. It was an innocent pastime, consuming and informative, but in some families it was forbidden as an invasion of other people's privacy. Young people in such families usually felt quite deprived and believed that they were the least-informed people in the community - which they probably were!

Certain rings would bring everyone onto the party line: a fire was signalled by one long, drawn-out ring, and immediately a chorus of voices could be heard anxiously asking where the fire was. The men would dash off as soon as they knew the location, to help their neighbours in this frightening emergency, and the women would begin preparing food to take to the site to feed the firefighters. In the case of a bush-fire, many men might have to spell each other off for days until the fire was brought under control, and the women would keep the food coming as long as it was needed. The fire would then be a major topic of telephone conversation in the community for weeks afterward.

Another popular and safe subject for telephone talk was the weather - which has always been and probably always will be a constant item of interest in a country that has such a changeable climate. Old people firmly believed that March always borrows a few days from April and returns them in the form of a few squally days in April. The telephone was usually installed in the big kitchen - the warmest and most convenient room in the farmhouse. Members of the family were usually working or sitting around close by and listening to at least one side of the conversation.

Crops and livestock were also frequent topics of telephone conversation: the birth of a calf and the fact that, although lambs are frequently born during a blizzard, a cow seldom gives birth during a severe storm, the best method of deflating a bloated cow, how the hens were laying, the yield of hay in the back field, the purchase or exchange of seed in the springtime were all matters to be shared with friends and neighbours over the telephone. Amusing anecdotes were often exchanged, perhaps like this one about a woman who had always kept a small flock of hens. She promised herself that she would donate to her church the money she earned from any eggs that were laid on Sundays. She vowed that from the time she made that decision, her hens laid more eggs on Sunday than on any other day of the week.

Household hints were shared by housewives in their telephone visits, farmers consulted each other on building or harvesting problems. Someone might offer the suggestion that a frightened dog could be restrained while porcupine quills were removed, by securing his head between the tongs of a hay fork, pressing the tips firmly into the ground. Mothers would discuss methods of treating a childhood disease, and neighbours would tell each other the latest news. The telephone brought people into much closer and regular touch with each other and changed the whole flavour of rural living.

While most people avoided discussing private subjects on the telephone because they never knew who might be listening along the party line, there were always a few who managed to insert a little gossip into the conversation. But nobody raised an eyebrow when someone announced, "Mrs. Jones is in bed with the doctor." That was not a bit of scandal; it merely meant that Mrs. Jones was sick and the doctor had visited, and prescribed a few days of bed rest - not an easy prescription to carry out when several children and many chores, both indoors and out, were awaiting her attention.

There was a way of insuring a more or less private conversation with another person on the same party line. Two people could agree beforehand to "come on the line" for a chat at a certain hour. They would pick up the receiver at the same time without ringing and thus without signalling to the neighbourhood that there was a conversation going on. This way of achieving some privacy was not completely foolproof, because someone could always pick up a receiver along the party line to make a call of his own. The would-be caller would usually ask "Is the line busy?" as a matter of common courtesy, in case a caller was waiting on the line for his party to respond to a call. Also, it was always possible that at the designated hour, others might be enjoying a telephone visit; usually two people making plans for a private call would take this possibility into account and arrange an alternate time for their chat.

In my own family, this type of prearranged chat was carried out by three young friends on the same party line, more or less successfully, for several years. As no great secret was ever revealed, privacy was not really that important - but the conspiracy for a private conversation brought a certain amount of excitement with it. Names that mattered were seldom revealed, but sometimes code phrases were used. "Was there a good crowd at the dance last night?" might really be a question about whether a certain special person had been present. The major topics of conversation during these three-way chats were school events, plans for social outings, and complicated arrangements for borrowing clothes back and forth.

To "call out" on the early telephones - that is, to call someone on another party line, or "long distance" - it was necessary to summon an operator at the central exchange. To do this the caller had to turn a crank and simultaneously press a button. If the finger were lifted inadvertently from the button while the right hand was still cranking, a "dingle" would be heard by all and sundry along the party line. This would inevitably bring a host of interested listeners onto the line, since a "call through central" naturally held more fascination than a simple call between neighbours.

"Central" - the name that was given to all the exchange operators - was expected to rise above and beyond the call of duty and was often assumed to be a mind reader. In the smaller exchanges, it sometimes seemed that she really was. Instead of putting a call through, she might tell the caller that his party was at the barbershop, or at a friend's house. In an emergency, she knew who to reach and where to find help. One youngster, wanting to call his aunt in the city, summoned the operator and asked simply, "Central, will you give me my Aunt Emma?"

It was a common practice, too, to call Central to check the correct time. My father was in the habit of doing this and one morning Central snapped back at him that she did not give out the time so early in the morning. "Central," he exclaimed, "I've been up for hours and have done half a day's work, and I don't know what time it is!" He got it.

Conclusion

"An ounce of prevention is worth a pound of cure" was a common expression in the days when medicines were often mixed and weighed in the home. Unfortunately, in too many instances, the measurements or weights were a case of by gosh or by golly, which, in fact, could spell kill or cure.

"People liberation" has always been on parallel with human compassion; my great grandfather, I have been told, rose very early to warm his good wife's cold corsets by the fire before she ventured forth from the cosy confines of her bed.

Youngsters became adept at changing clothes, without too many scorching incidents, behind the kitchen stove; several persons have recalled having dressed, as children under the heavy blankets and quilts which were piled high in frosty bedrooms when snow often filtered in at window corners and "the pot froze under the bed". Stovepipes came through some of the bedrooms and at close range offered a certain degree of warmth; clothes were often wrapped around the "black comforter" before being hastily changed.

"Laughter is the best medicine" we are told and it is unusual to find an old timer who lacks a sense of humour, albeit a dry one. They learned to take life as it came and became accustomed to pain, sorrow and set backs. They all seem to agree that hardships build character - and listening to their tales, we can't find argument with that.